AUDITS OF PUBLIC COMPANIES

AUDITS OF PUBLIC COMPANIES

GAO
REPORT

Nova Science Publishers, Inc.
New York

For permission to use material from this book please contact us:
Telephone 631-231-7269; Fax 631-231-8175
Web Site: http://www.novapublishers.com

LIBRARY OF CONGRESS CATALOGING-IN-PUBLICATION DATA

United States. General Accounting Office.
Audits of public companies / GAO.
p. cm.
ISBN 978-1-60456-503-4 (hbk.)
1. Accounting firms--United States. 2. Auditing--United States. 3. Corporations--United States--Auditing. I. Title.
HF5616.U5U55 2008
657'.450973--dc22 2008012775

Published by Nova Science Publishers, Inc. ✣ New York

CONTENTS

PREFACE[*]

This book examines (1) concentration in the market for public company audits, (2) the potential for smaller accounting firms' growth to ease market concentration, and (3) proposals that have been offered by others for easing concentration and the barriers facing smaller firms in expanding their market shares. This is an edited and excerpted version.

CONTINUED CONCENTRATION IN AUDIT MARKET FOR LARGE PUBLIC COMPANIES DOES NOT CALL FOR IMMEDIATE ACTION

WHY GAO DID THIS STUDY

GAO has prepared this report under the Comptroller General's authority as part of a continued effort to assist Congress in reviewing concentration in the market for public company audits. The small number of large international accounting firms performing audits of almost all large public companies raises interest in potential effects on competition and the choices available to large companies needing an auditor. This report examines (1) concentration in the market for public company audits, (2) the potential for smaller accounting firms' growth to ease market concentration, and (3) proposals that have been offered by others for easing concentration and the barriers facing smaller firms in expanding their market shares.

---

[*] Excerpted from GAO Report GAO-08-163, dated January 2008.

GAO surveyed a random sample of almost 600 large, medium, and small public companies on their experiences with their auditors. GAO also interviewed the four largest accounting firms and surveyed all other U.S. accounting firms that audit at least one public company. GAO also developed an econometric model that analyzed the extent to which various factors, including concentration and new auditing requirements, affected fee levels. To supplement this work, GAO interviewed market participants, including public companies, investors, accounting firms, academics, and regulators.

What GAO Found

While the small public company audit market is much less concentrated, the four largest accounting firms continue to audit almost all large public companies. According to GAO's survey, 82 percent of large public companies—the Fortune 1000—saw their choice of auditor as limited to three or fewer firms, and about 60 percent viewed competition in their audit market as insufficient. Most small public companies reported being satisfied with the auditor choices available to them.

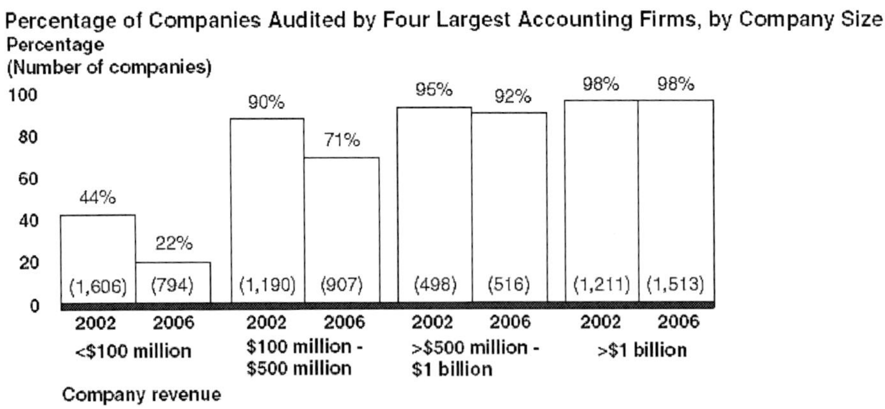

Source: GAO analysis of Audit Analytics data.

Figure. Percentage of Companies Audited by Four Largest Accounting Firms, by Company Size.

Although audit fees rose significantly in recent years, market participants attributed these increases to expanding accounting and auditing requirements and higher costs for accounting firm personnel. GAO's model also found that factors other than concentration appeared to explain audit fee levels. Public company officials generally acknowledged that audit quality had increased. Although current concentration does not appear to be having a significant adverse effect, the loss of another large firm would further reduce large companies' auditor choice and could affect audit fee competitiveness.

Smaller accounting firms face various challenges in expanding to audit more public companies, although most are not interested in these clients. As a result, concentration in the audit market for large public companies is likely to continue. Large public companies that GAO surveyed said that smaller firms lacked the capacity and technical expertise they wanted in an auditor. Audit firms that GAO surveyed said that adding qualified staff and increasing their name recognition were the most significant challenges they faced in expanding their public company audit practices. Some have taken steps to increase their capacity by joining networks with other firms.

Academics and business groups have put forth proposals to reduce audit market concentration and address challenges facing smaller accounting firms, including capping auditors' liability and creating an office to share technical expertise. Market participants raised questions about the overall effectiveness, feasibility, and benefit of these proposals, and none were widely supported. Given the lack of significant adverse effect of concentration in the current environment and that no clear consensus exists on how to reduce concentration, no compelling need for immediate action appears to exist.

Abbreviations

AICPA	American Institute of Certified Public Accountants
AMEX	American Stock Exchange
CAQ	Center for Audit Quality
CEO	chief executive officer
CFO	chief financial officer
CPA	certified public accountant
DOJ	Department of Justice
EDGAR	Electronic Data Gathering, Analysis, and Retrieval system
EITF	Emerging Issues Task Force
FASB	Financial Accounting Standards Board
FTC	Federal Trade Commission
GAAP	generally accepted accounting principles
GAAS	generally accepted auditing standards

GLS	generalized least squares
HHI	Hirschman-Herfindahl Index
IOSCO	International Organization of Securities Commissions
IPO	initial public offering
NAICS	North American Industry Classification System
NASBA	National Association of State Boards of Accountancy
NYSE	New York Stock Exchange
OLS	ordinary least squares
OTCBB	Over the Counter Bulletin Board
PAR	*Public Accounting Report*
PCAOB	Public Company Accounting Oversight Board
SEC	Securities and Exchange Commission

Public and investor confidence in the reliability of financial reporting is critical to the effective functioning of the U.S. capital markets. Federal securities laws require that a company raising capital by issuing securities to the public have an independent public accountant perform an audit of the company's financial statements to provide reasonable assurance about whether the financial statements are fairly presented. Since the 1980s, a small number of large U.S. accounting firms have traditionally performed audits for the vast majority of the public company market (when measured by the share of total audit fees collected). Among the clients of these large firms are almost all of the largest U.S. companies.[1] The small number of large accounting firms performing such audits has decreased as a result of mergers and the dissolution of one firm, falling from eight in the 1980s to four today.[2] These four firms—referred to here as the largest firms—have thousands of partners, tens of thousands of employees, offices located around the world, and each had more than one thousand public company audit clients for 2006.[3] The next four largest accounting firms—referred to here as midsize firms—operate nationally, and to some extent, internationally but have substantially fewer employees and partners, and each had less than 500 public company audit clients for 2006.[4] All other accounting firms—referred to here as smaller firms—audit regional and local public companies and have fewer than 100 public company clients.[5]

With the audit market concentrated among the four largest firms, concerns have been raised about the number of choices that companies have when selecting an auditor and the extent of competition in the market. In 2003, we conducted a study (mandated by the Sarbanes-Oxley Act) on consolidation that had occurred in the accounting profession. Our study followed the dissolution of one of the then-five largest accounting firms, Arthur Andersen. At that time, we found that although audits for large public companies were highly concentrated among the largest accounting firms, the market for audit services appeared competitive according to various indicators.[6] Given that several years have passed since the dissolution of Arthur Andersen and the passage of the Sarbanes-Oxley Act, which introduced reforms to public reporting and auditing, this report provides an update on the trends in the market for public company audits that we identified in 2003 in the market for public company audits.[7] Among the changes affecting the audit market that have occurred since our last report are additional requirements for public companies and auditors to assess, report on and attest to companies' internal control practices, restrictions intended to ensure the accounting firm's independence that limit public companies' ability to use their auditors for certain other services, and the creation of a new oversight body for accounting firms.

We prepared this report under the Comptroller General's authority to conduct evaluations on his own initiative as part of a continued effort to assist Congress in reviewing concentration in the market for public company audits. Specifically, this report examines (1) the level of concentration in the market for public company audits and the impact of this concentration, (2) the potential for increased capacity among midsize and smaller accounting firms to ease market concentration, and (3) proposals that have been offered by others for easing concentration in the market for public company audits and the barriers facing midsize and smaller firms in expanding their market share for public company audits.

To address these objectives, we collected data and analyzed changes in companies' choice of auditors and in audit fees, computed concentration ratios and other measures of concentration. We developed an econometric model to evaluate how various factors, including the level of market concentration, could explain fees that public companies paid to their auditors. To obtain the views of public companies and accounting firms on audit competition and challenges, we conducted two surveys. First, we surveyed a random sample of 595 of more than 6,000 publicly held companies, some of which had recently changed auditors.[8] Our sample included large public companies (those in the Fortune 1000); midsize public companies (those outside the Fortune 1000 with market capitalizations—the value of the total outstanding shares of stock—above $75 million); and small companies with less than $75 million in market capitalization.[9] Our response rate for this survey was 73 percent.[10] Because our survey was based on a random sample of the population, it is subject to sampling errors. The likely range of these errors for any survey statistics is no greater than plus or minus 12 percentage points, unless otherwise noted. In addition, we surveyed representatives of all 434 U.S. accounting firms that audited at least 1 public company in 2006 and were registered with the Public Company Accounting Oversight Board (PCAOB). Our response rate was 58 percent.[11] Results from our survey of accounting firms are limited to those midsize and smaller firms with five or more public company clients. Instead of surveying the four largest firms, we conducted separate structured interviews with representatives from each firm to obtain their views on the issues covered in the survey.

This report does not contain all the results from the surveys, but the surveys themselves and a more complete tabulation of the results can be viewed at http://www.gao.gov/cgi-bin/getrpt?GAO-08-164SP. We also interviewed staff from the Securities and Exchange Commission (SEC), PCAOB, Department of Justice (DOJ); academics; private consultants; trade associations; accounting firms; public companies; and insurance companies. To obtain information about the strengths and weaknesses of various proposals that have been offered to address concentration and the challenges that midsize and smaller firms face, we also held a roundtable discussion on July 10, 2007, involving 18 market participants, including representatives of accounting firms, public companies, investors, academics, and insurers. For more information on our scope and methodology, see appendix I.

We conducted this performance audit in New York City and Washington, D.C., from October 2006 to January 2008 in accordance with generally accepted government auditing standards. Those standards require that we plan and perform the audit to obtain sufficient, appropriate evidence to provide a reasonable basis for our findings and conclusions based on our audit objectives. We believe that the evidence obtained provides a reasonable basis for our findings and conclusions based on our audit objectives.

Chapter 1

RESULTS IN BRIEF

Although the market for small public company audits has become much less concentrated since 2002, the continuing concentration in the market for larger public companies limits these companies' auditor choices but does not appear to have significantly affected audit fees. According to our analysis, the largest accounting firms audit 98 percent of the more than 1,500 largest public companies—those with annual revenues of more than $1 billion. In contrast, midsize and smaller firms audit almost 80 percent of the more than 3,600 smallest companies—those with annual revenues of less than $100 million. Larger public companies we surveyed indicated that the industry expertise and technical capability that they sought in an auditor generally meant that their choices were limited to the largest accounting firms. According to our survey of a random sample drawn from a population of more than 6,000 public companies, almost 60 percent of large companies indicated that the number of accounting firms from which they could choose was not adequate, although some company officials described taking steps to ensure that they would have at least one alternative firm they could use under the more restrictive auditor independence rules. In contrast, about 75 percent of the smallest public companies saw their number of auditor choices as sufficient. While audit fees have increased significantly in recent years, many market participants that we interviewed attributed fee increases to additional audit work and expanded accounting and audit requirements and higher costs to hire, train, and retain qualified staff. In addition, the econometric model we developed to evaluate the relationship between market concentration and audit fees indicated that factors other than concentration appeared to explain the recent fee increases. The level of market concentration also does not appear to be affecting audit quality as many of our survey respondents and those we interviewed said that audit quality had improved, which some attributed to the Sarbanes-Oxley Act. Although the current level of concentration does not appear to be having significant adverse effect, public company officials and others we interviewed indicated that a merger or the failure of one of the largest firms would further reduce companies' auditor choices and could potentially result in higher audit fees and fewer choices. The various federal organizations that have a role in overseeing activities in the audit market, including SEC, PCAOB, and DOJ, are prepared to take various actions to help minimize the disruption to the market if further concentration occurred.

The concentration in the large public company audit market is also unlikely to be reduced in the near term by midsize and smaller accounting firms because a significant majority is not interested in auditing large public companies and those that are interested face various challenges in expanding their capability to do so. Over 70 percent of midsize and smaller accounting firms indicated that they were not attempting to obtain large public company clients. Approximately 90 percent of large public companies we surveyed cited lack of capacity as a reason why they would not consider using midsize or smaller firms as their auditor. As a result, many of these firms would have to greatly expand their staffing and geographic capabilities to serve such companies. However, the most frequent impediment to expansion cited by accounting firms responding to our survey was difficulty finding staff. Smaller firms also saw their lack of name recognition and reputation as preventing them from obtaining more large public company clients. Other difficulties that some accounting firms cited in obtaining more public company clients included limited access to capital and difficulty complying with multiple state licensing requirements. Some firms have taken steps to address such challenges, such as mergers or joining networks.

Various proposals by academics and business groups have been put forth to reduce the risks of current and further audit market concentration and the challenges facing midsize and smaller accounting firms, but each proposal also has disadvantages. For example, some have suggested that requiring one or more of the largest firms to spin off a portion of their operations to create more than four firms with the capacity to audit large public companies could ease current concentration. However, market participants we spoke with raised concerns that splitting up these firms could reduce their economies of scale and the depth of expertise that currently allow the largest firms to effectively and efficiently audit large companies. Some have also put forth proposals to reduce the risk of further concentration that could arise if one of the largest firms leaves the market as the result of a large litigation judgment or a regulatory action. Proposals to reduce this risk include placing caps on auditors' liability and having regulators or others take enforcement actions only against responsible partners or employees rather than the firm as whole. However, some of the academics and others we spoke with saw such liability caps and enforcement limitations as potentially reducing the incentives for auditors to conduct quality work. Other proposals have been offered to help midsize and smaller firms expand their market share, thus potentially easing concentration. These proposals include allowing outside ownership of these firms in order to provide capital to expand their operations, creating a group of accounting and auditing experts to provide needed expertise to smaller auditing firms, and establishing a professionwide accreditation program to help these firms overcome some of the name recognition and reputation challenges they face. However, while each action could offer benefits, market participants generally saw these proposals as having limited effectiveness, feasibility, and benefit.

In light of limited evidence that the currently concentrated market for large public company audits has created significant adverse impact and the general lack of any proposals that were clearly seen as effective in addressing the risks of concentration or challenges facing smaller firms without serious drawbacks, we found no compelling need to take action. As a result, this report does not include any recommendations. We provided copies of a draft of this report to SEC, DOJ, PCAOB, and the Department of the Treasury. SEC, PCAOB, and DOJ provided technical comments, which have been incorporated where appropriate. Treasury had no comments.

Chapter 2

BACKGROUND

Following the 1929 stock market crash, legislation was passed that required companies seeking to raise funds from the public to provide audited financial statements to their investors. The Securities Act of 1933 and the Securities Exchange Act of 1934 established the principle of full disclosure, which requires that public companies provide full and accurate information to the investing public. Under these federal securities laws, public companies are responsible for the preparation and content of financial statements that are complete and accurate and are presented in conformity with U.S. generally accepted accounting principles (GAAP). Financial statements, which disclose a company's financial position (balance sheet), stockholders' equity, results of operations (income statement), and cash flows, are an essential component of the disclosure system on which the U.S. capital and credit markets are based.

Federal securities laws also require that public companies have the financial statements they prepare audited by an independent public accountant. The independent public accountant's audit is critical to the financial reporting process because the audit subjects companies' financial statements to scrutiny on behalf of shareholders and creditors to whom company management is accountable. The auditor is the independent link between management and those who rely on the financial statements. The statutory independent audit requirement, in effect, grants a franchise to the nation's public accountants, as an audit opinion on a public company's financial statements must be secured before an issuer of securities can go to market, have the securities listed on the nation's stock exchanges, or comply with the reporting requirements of the securities laws.

Having auditors attest to the reliability of financial statements of public companies is intended to increase public and investor confidence in the fairness of the financial information. Moreover, investors and other users of financial statements expect auditors to bring integrity, independence, objectivity, and professional competence to the financial reporting process and to prevent the issuance of misleading financial statements. The resulting sense of confidence in companies' audited financial statements, which is key to the efficient functioning of the markets for public companies' securities, can exist only if reasonable investors perceive auditors as independent and expert professionals who will conduct thorough audits. In the event that companies are alleged to have misled the public or presented falsified financial information, the accounting firms that performed those audits are also sometimes included in suits brought by investors or actions pursued by regulators.

Accounting Firm Structure

Most accounting firms that audit public companies in the United States are organized as partnerships. Unlike corporations, which generally issue stock to their shareholders in exchange for capital to conduct their operations, accounting firms structured as partnerships obtain capital from their partners. To conduct an audit of a public company, an accounting firm establishes an engagement team that is typically headed by a lead audit partner and includes a concurring audit partner, audit staff and managers, and, as needed, technical specialists. The lead audit partner has responsibility for decision making on significant auditing, accounting, and reporting matters that affect the financial statements; reviewing the audit work; and maintaining regular contact with management and the audit committee. The concurring audit partner is responsible for reviewing the audit.[12]

To provide technical assistance to engagement teams, the larger accounting firms have national offices staffed with experts in auditing and accounting standards. These national offices are made up of accounting and auditing technical specialists who assist engagement teams by responding to complex questions, researching answers, and providing guidance to individual audit teams. These specialists also provide guidance to the entire firm on handling issues that arise during the course of audits, including evaluating the fair presentation of the financial statements.

MERGERS AND THE LOSS OF A MAJOR FIRM HAVE RESULTED IN A NATIONAL AND INTERNATIONAL MARKET DOMINATED BY FOUR LARGE FIRMS

Although the largest U.S. accounting firms have used mergers and acquisitions to help build their businesses and expand nationally and internationally since the early part of the twentieth century, in the late 1980s the eight largest firms—known as the Big 8—began merging with each other. As shown in figure 1, by 2000 various mergers among the largest accounting firms had left five large firms that accounted for the majority of audit revenues among firms auditing public companies.

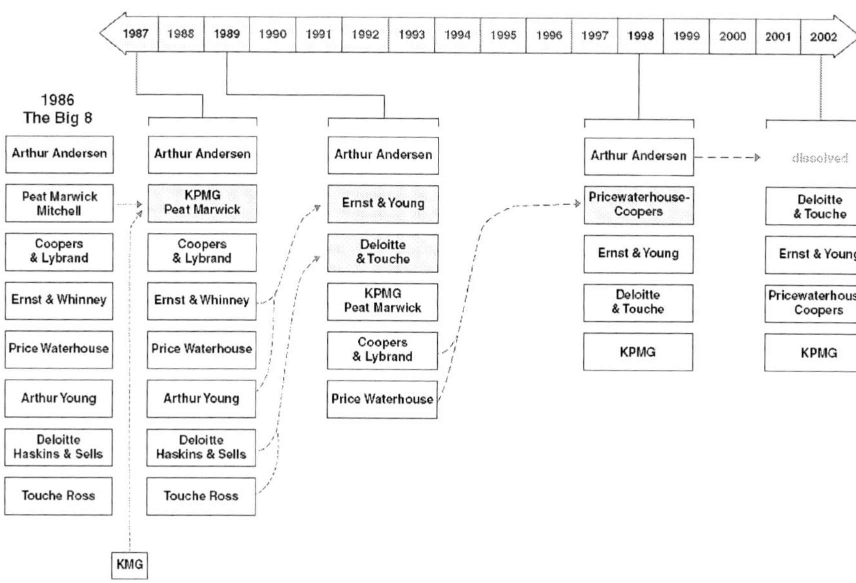

Sources: Interviews with the four largest accounting firms and *Public Accounting Report*, 1986-2002.

Figure 1. Significant Mergers of the 1980s and 1990s.

In 2002, the market consolidated further to 4 large firms after the Department of Justice criminally indicted Arthur Andersen on obstruction of justice charges stemming from the firm's role as auditor of Enron Corporation. The indictment and subsequent conviction of Arthur Andersen led to a mass exodus of its partners and staff, as well as clients. As a result, the firm was dissolved in 2002.[13]

Statutory Changes Affecting Requirements for Public Companies and Their Auditors

Public companies and the accounting profession have experienced many reporting and auditing changes in recent years. In the aftermath of various financial scandals at large public companies such as Enron and WorldCom in the early 2000s, new legislation was passed to help restore investor confidence in the nation's capital markets.[14] The Sarbanes-Oxley Act of 2002 (the Act) introduced major reforms to public company financial reporting and auditing that were intended to improve the accuracy and reliability of financial reporting and enhance auditors' independence and audit quality. The reforms include the following:

- Section 404(a) of the Act requires that in each annual financial report filed with SEC the management of public companies must (1) state its responsibility for establishing and maintaining an adequate internal control structure and procedures for financial reporting and (2) assess the effectiveness of its internal control structure and procedures for financial reporting.
- Section 404(b) requires that each public company's accounting firm must attest to and report on management's assessment of the effectiveness of internal control over financial reporting.
- A separate provision prohibits the company's auditor from providing certain nonaudit services, including bookkeeping, appraisal services, actuarial services, and internal audit outsourcing services.
- Another provision requires the mandatory rotation of lead and reviewing audit partners after they have provided audit services to a particular public company for 5 consecutive years.

The Act also established the PCAOB as a private-sector nonprofit organization subject to SEC oversight. PCAOB's mission is to oversee the audits of public companies in order to protect the interests of investors and further the public interest in the preparation of informative, fair, and independent audit reports. Table 1 shows other provisions affecting the corporate governance, auditing, and financial reporting of public companies.

Table 1. Summary of Selected Sarbanes-Oxley Act Provisions Affecting Public Companies and Accounting Firms

Provision	Main requirements
Section 101: Public Company Accounting Oversight Board	Establishes the PCAOB to oversee the audit of public companies that are subject to the securities laws.
Section 201: Services Outside the Scope of Practice of Auditors	Registered accounting firms cannot provide certain nonaudit services to a public company if the firm also serves as the auditor of the financial statements for the public company. Examples of prohibited nonaudit services include bookkeeping, appraisal or valuation services, internal audit outsourcing services, and management functions.
Section 301: Public Company Audit Committees	Listed company audit committees are responsible for the appointment, compensation, and oversight of the registered accounting firm, including the resolution of disagreements between the registered accounting firm and company management regarding financial reporting. Audit committee members must be independent.
Section 302: Corporate Responsibility for Financial Reports	For each annual and quarterly report filed with SEC, the chief executive officer (CEO) and chief financial officer (CFO) must certify that they have reviewed the report and, based on their knowledge, the report does not contain untrue statements or omissions of a material fact resulting in a misleading report and that, based on their knowledge, the financial information in the report is presented fairly.
Section 404: Management Assessment of Internal Controls	This section consists of two parts (a and b). First, in each annual report filed with SEC, company management must state its responsibility for establishing and maintaining an adequate internal control structure and procedures for financial reporting, and assess the effectiveness of its internal control structure and procedures for financial reporting. Second, the registered accounting firm must attest to, and report on, management's assessment of the effectiveness of its internal control over financial reporting.
Section 407: Disclosure of Audit Committee Financial Expert	Public companies must disclose in periodic reports to SEC whether the audit committee includes at least one member who is a financial expert and, if not, the reasons why.

Source: GAO.

The PCAOB has several responsibilities, including

- registering public accounting firms that prepare audit reports for public companies;
- establishing auditing, quality control, ethics, independence, and other standards relating to the preparation of audit reports for public companies;
- conducting inspections of registered public accounting firms; and

- conducting investigations and disciplinary proceedings of registered public accounting firms and those associated with such firms.

Under the Act, SEC was granted oversight and enforcement authority over PCAOB and must approve rules proposed by PCAOB for them to become effective.[15]

PCAOB is required to annually inspect registered accounting firms that provide audit reports for more than 100 issuers and at least triennially inspect firms with fewer issuers.[16] It conducted its first accounting firm inspections during 2003, but these inspections were limited in scope and were performed only on the largest firms. Since 2004, PCAOB has conducted full scope inspections of accounting firms of all sizes. As required in the Sarbanes-Oxley Act, PCAOB has issued individual reports to the accounting firms explaining issues identified in the inspections and has also issued reports covering common observations from their inspection process.[17]

The Sarbanes-Oxley Act also mandated that we study (1) the factors contributing to the mergers among the largest accounting firms in the 1980s and 1990s; (2) the implications of consolidation on competition and client choice, audit fees, audit quality, and auditor independence; (3) the effect of consolidation on capital formation and securities markets; and (4) barriers to entry faced by smaller accounting firms in competing with the largest firms for large public company audits. In 2003, we issued our report *Public Accounting Firms: Mandated Study on Consolidation and Competition* (GAO-03-864). We concluded in 2003 that the audit market was in the midst of unprecedented change. The market had become more highly concentrated, and the largest firms, as well as other accounting firms, faced tremendous challenges as they adapted to new risks and responsibilities, new independence standards, a new business model, and a new oversight structure, among other things. In many cases it was unclear what the ultimate outcome of the changes would be, and we noted that past findings might not reflect the future situation. We also identified several important issues that we believed warranted additional attention and study by the appropriate regulatory or enforcement agencies, such as the effect of the existing level of concentration on audit price and quality.

SIGNIFICANT AUDIT AND ACCOUNTING STANDARDS AND RULES CHANGES SINCE 2003

Since 2003, significant activity related to management reporting and auditing standards has continued to occur. In 2002, 2003, and 2004, SEC issued rules and guidance on implementing some of the Sarbanes-Oxley Act's provisions. Among these was the requirement that a public company's chief executive officer and chief financial officer certify in quarterly and annual reports issued after August 29, 2002, that their company's financial statements fairly present in material respects the company's financial condition (Section 302).[18] In June 2003, SEC issued final rules to implement Section 404 of the Sarbanes-Oxley Act.[19] Section 404(a) requires company management, in each annual report filed with SEC, to state their responsibility for establishing and maintaining an adequate internal control structure and procedures for financial reporting and to assess the effectiveness of its internal control structure and procedures for financial reporting. Section 404(b), which requires the registered accounting firm to attest to and report on management's assessment of the effectiveness of its internal control over financial reporting was implemented later. Public companies whose outstanding stock held by the public was valued at $75 million or more—known as accelerated filers—were first required to comply with Section 404(a) and (b) for fiscal years ending on or after November 15, 2004.[20] Public companies with stock in public hands valued at less than $75 million—called nonaccelerated filers—were granted several extensions but are now expected to comply with these Section 404 requirements over the next 2 years—for Section 404(a) in fiscal years ending after December 15, 2007, and for Section 404(b) in the first annual filing after December 15, 2008.

PCAOB issued its first audit standard on December 17, 2003, which the SEC approved on May 14, 2004, and, as of August 2007, has issued a total of five audit standards. On July 25, 2007, SEC approved Auditing Standard No. 5, *An Audit of Internal Control Over Financial Reporting That is Integrated with an Audit of Financial Statements*, to replace Auditing Standard No. 2, *An Audit of Internal Control Over Financial Reporting Performed in Conjunction with an Audit of Financial Statements*. According to PCAOB, Auditing Standard No. 2 was more costly than expected, and the related effort involved in complying with it appeared to be more than was necessary to conduct an effective audit of internal controls over financial reporting. Specifically, PCAOB noted that auditors were focusing on minutiae that were unlikely to affect the financial statements and that audit programs were not tailored to small companies. Auditing Standard No. 5, which is expected to address some of the cost issues, became effective for audits in fiscal years ending on or after November 15, 2007.

Other accounting and financial reporting standards and requirements have been implemented in recent years. Between January 2003 and August 2007, the Financial Accounting Standards Board (FASB), which issues the accounting standards that SEC recognizes as GAAP for public companies, issued 11 statements (Nos. 149 through 159) and revised statement number 123. These statements cover a range of topics including financial instruments, fair value, and pensions. In addition, other guidance has been issued by the FASB emerging issues task force (EITF), SEC, and other groups. For instance, FASB issued EITF Issue No. 06-6, "Debtor's Accounting for a Modification (or Exchange) of Convertible Debt Instruments" in November 2006. SEC issued Staff Accounting Bulletin Number 108 on September 13, 2006, summarizing the views of the staff regarding the process of quantifying financial statement misstatements.

These recent changes to accounting and financial reporting standards and guidance add to an already highly complex set of standards and rules for public company financial reporting. Currently GAAP consists of more than 2,000 separate pronouncements issued in various forms by numerous bodies including SEC, FASB, American Institute of Certified Public Accountants (AICPA), and others. SEC Chairman Cox has stated that "our current system of financial reporting has become unnecessarily complex for investors, companies, and the markets generally."[21] In June 2007, SEC established the SEC Advisory Committee on Improvements to Financial Reporting to study the causes of complexity and recommend ways to make financial reports clearer and more beneficial to investors, reduce costs and unnecessary burdens for preparers, and better use advances in technology to enhance all aspects of financial reporting.

Chapter 3

With Continued Audit Market Concentration, Large Public Companies See Limited Choices, but No Apparent Significant Effect on Fees

Despite some reduction since 2002, the overall public company audit market has remained highly concentrated. For large public companies, the market remains highly concentrated, with the four largest accounting firms auditing the financial statements of almost all large public companies. However, the audit market for smaller public companies has become much less concentrated since 2002. Larger public companies indicated that the industry expertise and technical capability that they sought in an auditor generally meant that their choices were limited to the largest accounting firms in this highly concentrated market. Those we spoke to and surveyed had mixed views on the extent to which the current level of concentration adversely affected choice, audit prices, and audit quality, but most participants did not see the current level of concentration as significantly affecting these aspects of competition. Although audit fees have increased and public companies' opinions of the adequacy of competition in the audit market varied, other factors appear to explain the recent fee increases. While the current level of concentration does not appear to be having significant adverse effect, the loss of another of the larger firms would further increase concentration and limit company choices and may affect price competition. Regulators overseeing the functioning of the audit market could take several actions in response to another large audit firm's leaving the market.

Overall Market for Public Company Audits Remains Highly Concentrated

To assess the degree of concentration in a market, we used the preferred practice of examining the proportion of each competing seller's—in this case accounting firms—share of the overall revenue collected. In the case of accounting firms, the revenue measured is the total amount of fees these firms collected. Using data from Audit Analytics, which collects audit fee information from the filings public companies submit to SEC, we found that the largest firms collected 94 percent of all audit fees paid by public companies in 2006, slightly less than the 96 percent they collected in 2002. As a result, the overall market continues to represent a tight oligopoly, which is a concentrated market in which a small number of firms have large enough market share to potentially use their market power, either unilaterally or through collusion, to greatly influence price and other business practices to their advantage.[22]

A key statistical measure used to assess market concentration and the potential for firms to exercise market power is the Hirschman-Herfindahl Index (HHI).[23] The HHI for a market is calculated using the various market shares (in the case of the audit market, measured by total audit fees collected) of all the firms competing to offer services within that market. In 2006, the HHI for the overall market for public company audits was 2,300. According to guidelines issued jointly by the Department of Justice (DOJ) and the Federal Trade Commission (FTC), an HHI above 1,800 indicates a highly concentrated market. Analyzing the audit market by industry and region reveals that many industries have similarly highly concentrated audit markets. For example, in 2006 the HHI of the audit market in the utilities sector was over 3,500. The audit market was also similarly concentrated for companies across six major geographic regions of the country.[24] (App. II contains further discussion of overall market concentration.)

In addition to the potential for dominant competitors to use their market power to charge uncompetitive prices, highly concentrated markets also raise other competitive concerns. For example, firms with significant market power have the potential to reduce the quality of their products or to cut back on the services they provide because the lack of competitive alternatives would limit customers' ability to obtain services elsewhere. Similarly, firms that dominate a given market may feel less pressure to introduce innovative products and services. Finally, a highly concentrated market increases the potential for the dominant firms to engage in coordinated actions that can harm clients, such as coordinating actions to influence the development of standards that raise costs for their customers. However, the presence of high market shares does not necessarily mean that anticompetitive behavior is occurring. Competition in an oligopoly can also be intense and result in a market with competitive prices, innovation, and high-quality products.

Markets with a few large dominant firms can form for natural reasons and can also be beneficial. As we reported in 2003, several key factors spurred the increased consolidation in the market that resulted from the mergers of the eight largest accounting firms in the 1980s and 1990s.[25] For example, as U.S. corporations have increasingly expanded into global markets, their need for accounting firms with greater global reach also increased. Many public companies have developed more complex operations and financial transactions, such as the increasing use of derivatives and other financial arrangements, and these changes increased the need for auditors with specialized industry-specific or technical expertise.

Further, some accounting firms wanted to modernize their operations, build their staff capacity, and spread their risk over a broader capital base, and large firms can achieve greater economies of scale by spreading certain fixed costs, such as staff training, over an expanded client base. Therefore, the size of the largest firms may enable them to develop sufficient technical expertise and the ability to conduct work globally to meet the needs of complex multinational audit clients and to do so at a lower cost than could be provided by smaller audit firms. Some academic sources have also suggested that the size of the largest firms may give them the ability to resist potential pressure from large public company clients to reduce or compromise audit quality.

Although Smaller Public Company Market Has Become Less Concentrated, Concentration in the Market for Large Companies Persists

Although the market is concentrated overall, the degree of market concentration, and, thus, the extent to which the largest firms dominate, declines with the size of public companies. As shown in figure 2, the proportion of large public companies audited by one of the largest accounting firms has not changed since 2002. However, the proportion of the smallest public companies that used the largest auditors fell by half from 2002 to 2006. Specifically, the share of public companies with less than $100 million in revenue audited by the largest firms decreased from 44 percent to 22 percent over this period. As figure 2 shows, smaller accounting firms now serve as auditors for many of the companies that had previously used the largest firms. The share of companies with revenues between $100 and $500 million that the largest firms audited also declined during this period from 90 to 71 percent. Officials from the largest accounting firms and other market participants told us resource constraints in the aftermath of the Arthur Andersen collapse and the Sarbanes-Oxley Act led the largest firms to resign from auditing some smaller companies or raised their audit fees higher than some smaller companies were willing to pay.

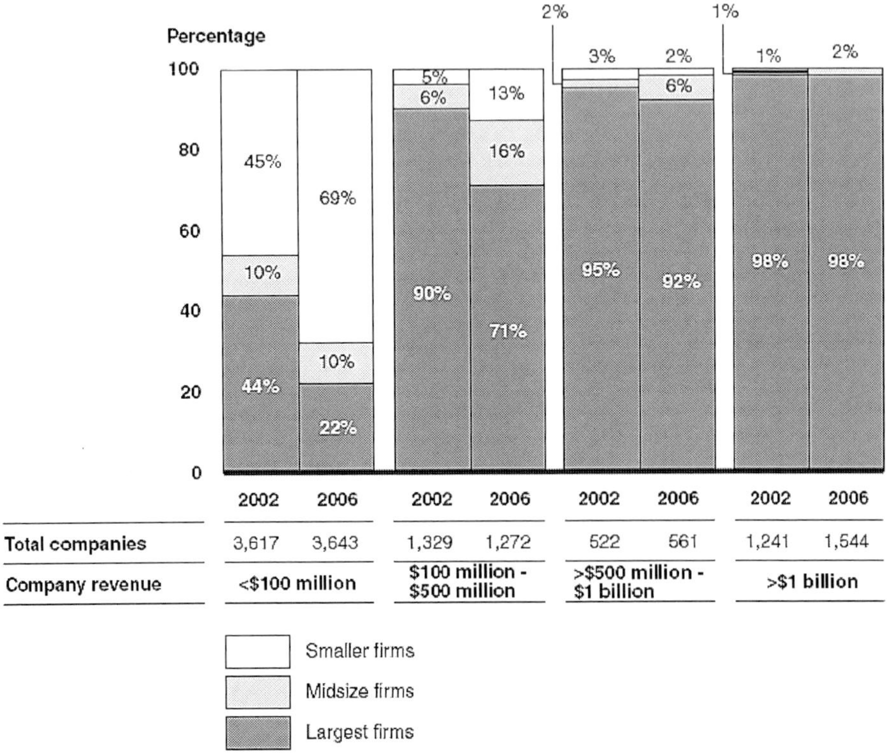

Source: GAO analysis of Audit Analytics data.

Note: Totals do not always add to 100 percent due to rounding.

Figure 2. Public Companies and Their Auditors, 2002 and 2006.

As the share of smaller companies audited by the largest firms has declined, concentration in the audit market for these companies has eased significantly. By grouping public companies by their revenues and calculating HHIs for these groupings, we found that while the audit market for larger public companies with revenues greater than $500 million remained highly concentrated, the market for smaller public companies with 500 million in revenue or less had become much less concentrated.[26] As figure 3 shows, between 2002 and 2006 the HHI for the audit market for the smallest public companies—those with annual revenues of less than $100 million—declined from a level of 1,400 to about 800. According to DOJ and FTC guidelines, a market with an HHI of less than 1000 is considered to be unconcentrated, and no competitor would likely have the ability to exert market power. The audit market for public companies with revenues between $100 million and $500 million also became less concentrated. The HHI for this market fell from a 2002 level indicating high concentration to a 2006 level indicating only moderate concentration.

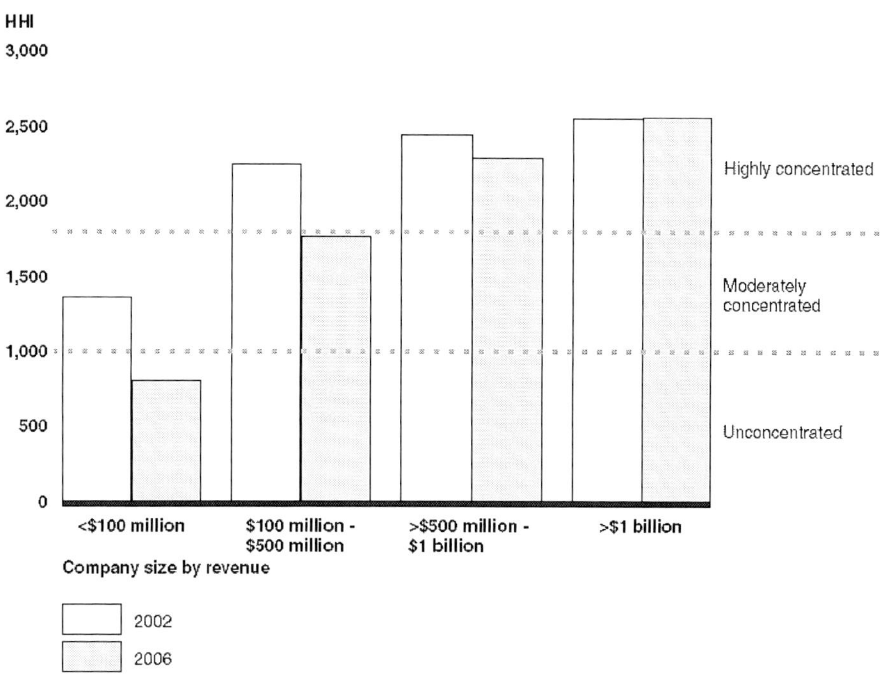

Source: GAO analysis of Audit Analytics data.

Figure 3. Hirschman-Herfindahl Indexes for Public Company Market Segments Grouped by Company Revenues.

In Concentrated Market, Some Companies Perceive Limited Auditor Choice

Many of the largest public companies—those in the Fortune 1000—told us that they generally found the audit firm attributes they sought only in the largest accounting firms, and as a result, many of these companies saw their number of auditor choices as insufficient. Midsize and small companies were generally more likely than large companies to report that they had more than three choices.

Large Public Companies and Auditor Choices

In the current concentrated market, large companies perceived their choices as limited, in part because these companies generally said, if they had to choose a new auditor, they were not likely to use accounting firms smaller than the largest firms.[27] Our survey of the audit committee chairs of almost 600 public companies based in the United States showed that 86 percent of large public companies in the Fortune 1000 were not likely to use a midsize accounting firm and that none were likely to use a smaller accounting firm as a new auditor of record.[28] In explaining their position, these companies most frequently cited the auditor's ability to handle the size and complexity of their company's operations as being of great or very great importance (92 percent). In addition, 80 percent cited the auditor's technical capability with accounting principles and auditing standards and 67 percent cited the need for industry specialization or expertise as of great or very great importance as reasons why they would not consider a midsize or smaller auditor. Similarly, in interviews and comments on our survey, some company officials noted that they chose the largest firms because they believed that these firms had the attributes the company needed, while midsize and smaller firms did not. For example, the audit committee chair of one large company commented that the company would not choose a midsize or smaller auditor because the company's industry was very complex, and, therefore, the company needed an auditor with specific industry experience. The chief financial officer (CFO) of another large public company noted that because of the company's size and international operations, the largest firms were the only viable options.

The need to comply with independence standards and other factors can further limit the number of choices available to large public companies for their auditor of record. As required under the Sarbanes-Oxley Act, SEC rules, and auditing standards, a company's auditor must be independent. Public companies are prohibited from obtaining audits from firms that also provide the company with certain nonaudit services, including bookkeeping, design and implementation of financial information systems, valuation services, and internal audit outsourcing services.[29] Ninety-six percent of large companies reported that they used one of the largest firms for some nonaudit services, potentially further reducing the number of choices for their auditor of record if they are precluded from using those firms due to independence rules. According to our survey data, 27 percent of large public companies that had not switched auditors since 2003 reported that the independence restrictions on using certain firms were of at least some importance in deciding to retain their current auditor, although only 9 percent listed these restrictions as of great or very great importance.[30]

In interviews, officials from a few large public companies indicated that they maintained options while remaining in compliance with independence requirements by not using at least one of the largest firms for prohibited nonaudit services, in some cases by using smaller firms for these services. In this way, they hoped to ensure that they would have at least one independent firm to choose if they had to change auditors. Some interviewees we spoke with suggested that companies using only the largest firms for both audit and nonaudit services could be unnecessarily limiting their choices because many midsize and smaller firms were capable of handling certain nonaudit services.

A few companies may feel constrained in their choice of auditors for other reasons. For example, some companies' desire to avoid using a competitor's auditor can reduce the number of choices they have, according to several industry participants. However, over 90 percent of the large companies that responded to our 2003 survey were willing to choose a firm as their auditor regardless of whether that firm also audited a competitor.[31] Further, some market participants and regulators noted that in certain industries, large public companies may have more limited choices because one or more of the largest firms was not very active in those industries. For example, in 2006 one of the largest firms held 77 percent of the market for public company audits in the agriculture, forestry, fishing, and hunting industry, while another of the largest firms had only a 1 percent market share.[32]

Consistent with reporting that they were not likely to use midsize and smaller audit firms, large companies also indicated that they had a limited number of firms to choose from, and many believed that this number was generally insufficient. According to our survey, about 80 percent of large public companies said that they would have three or fewer accounting firms (other than their current auditor of record) to choose from if they needed to change primary auditors. The proportion of large companies that reported having three or fewer choices was about the same for both domestic and multinational companies. Furthermore, over half (57 percent) of large public companies stated that the number of accounting firms that they could choose among was not adequate.[33] Forty-three percent of large public companies that responded to the survey we conducted for our 2003 report indicated that they had insufficient choices for an auditor of record.

Large public companies' preference for the largest audit firms was illustrated by the firms these companies choose when they changed auditors. Although some public companies maintain their relationships with the same audit firm for many years, there were almost 6,000 changes in auditors between 2003 and 2007. We analyzed data from Audit Analytics and found that 102 large companies had changed auditors between January 1, 2003, and June 30, 2007.[34] Of the 95 large companies that were previously audited by one of the largest firms, 88 (93 percent) of these companies changed from one of the largest auditors to another of the largest auditors. Only seven switched to a midsize auditor. The remaining seven large companies that changed auditors during this period had been previously audited by a midsize or smaller auditor, but switched to one of the largest firms. (App. III shows more analysis of the data on auditor changes and the reasons these companies reported for changing auditors.)

Midsize and Small Public Companies and Auditor Choices

Although many midsize public companies reported that their choice of auditors was limited, smaller companies generally reported having more choices than larger companies, if they had to change auditors. For example, among midsize companies, 59 percent of multinational and 52 percent of domestic companies reported that their choices were limited to three or fewer firms (figure 4). In contrast, only about one-third (34 percent) of small companies indicated that they were restricted to three or fewer accounting firms and over 40 percent said that they had six or more choices.

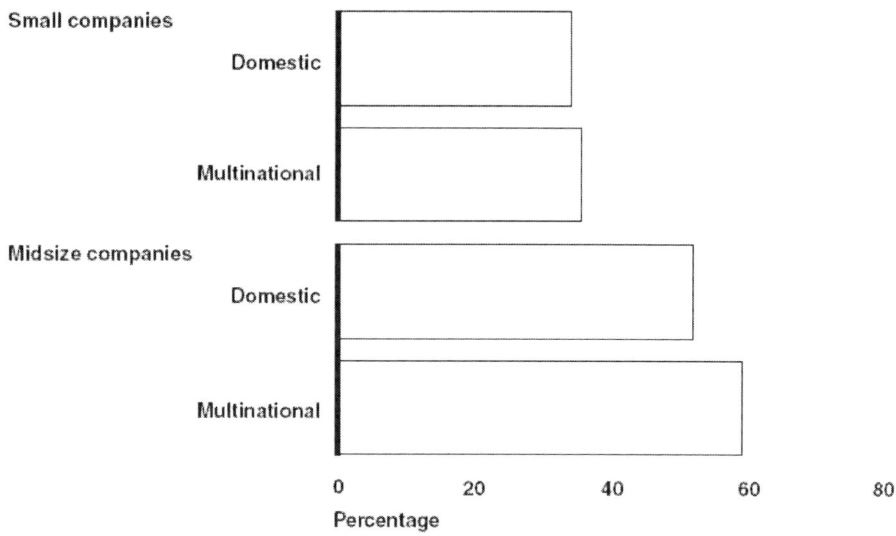

Source: GAO.

Note: The estimate for small multinational companies is subject to a sampling error of +/- 16 percentage points.

Figure 4. Percentage of Midsize and Small Companies That Reported Having Three or Fewer Choices for Auditor.

Based on our survey, midsize and small public companies were more likely than large companies to consider using midsize or smaller accounting firms if they had to choose a new auditor. About half (51 percent) of midsize companies would consider using midsize firms and 16 percent would consider using smaller firms. Further, 74 percent of small public companies would consider using smaller firms.

In addition, compared with large companies, more midsize and small companies were satisfied with the number of choices they had for possible auditors. As shown in figure 5, about half of midsize and less than a fifth of small companies reported that the number of choices they had was not enough.

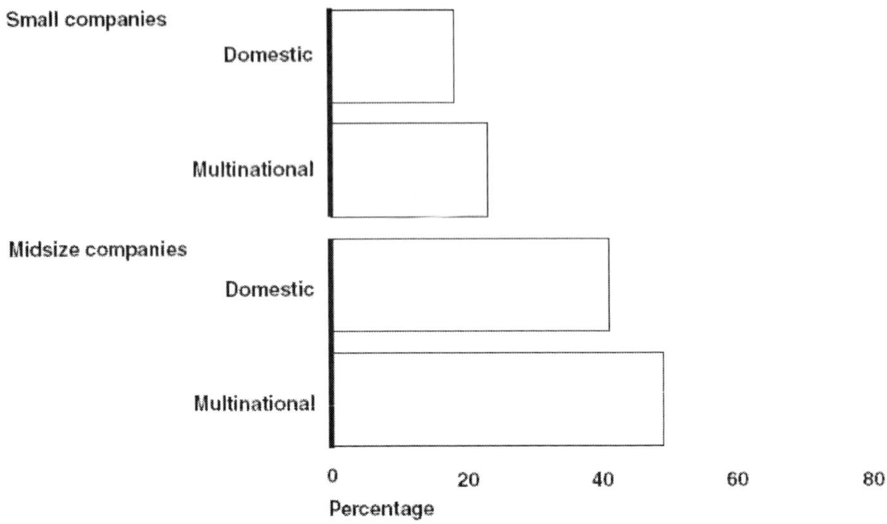

Source: GAO.

Note: The estimate for small multinational companies is subject to a sampling error of +/- 14 percentage points.

Figure 5. Percentage of Small and Midsize Companies Reporting They Did Not Have Enough Choices for Auditor.

However, about 60 percent of midsize multinational companies reported that they would have three or fewer choices if they had to change auditors and about half said the number of choices was not enough.

Our analysis also showed that many midsize and small public companies have moved to midsize or smaller auditors. Since 2003, over 1,400 midsize and small companies that had been audited by one of the largest firms have changed auditors. Of these, almost 1,100 (about 74 percent) engaged midsize or smaller firms as their new auditors and about 360 (about 25 percent) chose another one of the largest auditors (figure 6). In contrast, only 13 percent of midsize and small companies that left midsize auditors and 3 percent of midsize and small companies that left smaller auditors subsequently engaged one of the largest firms.

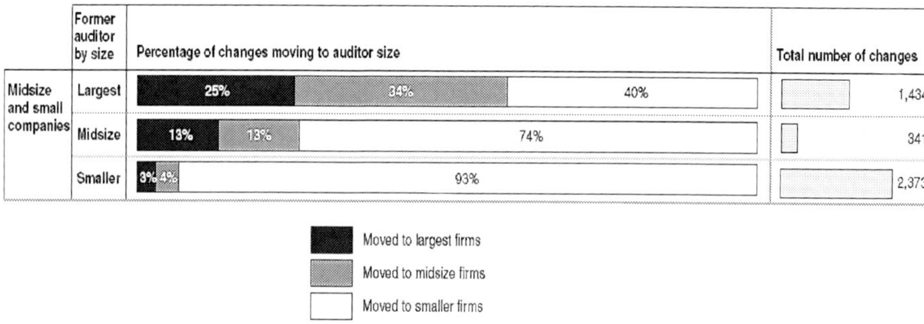

Source: GAO analysis of Audit Analytics data.

Figure 6. Changes in Auditors among Small and Midsize Public Companies.

Although Opinions on the Impact of Concentration in the Large Public Company Market Varied, Other Factors Appeared to Account for Recent Fee Increases

Opinions varied on the effect of concentration on competition and on the sufficiency of competition in the market for public company audits. Many of the market participants we interviewed felt that competition was quite strong and not significantly affected by concentration. For example, representatives of the largest firms told us that they competed intensely with each other. Some of the public company officials we spoke with also saw the audit market as competitive. For example, the audit committee chair of one large public company said that although a major competitor was lost when Arthur Andersen dissolved, the market had adjusted and was still competitive. However, several companies we surveyed commented that, with few firms to choose from, the market did not have enough competition. For example, the CFO of a midsize company said that consolidation in the market had led to a decline of value-added services by auditors and an escalation of audit pricing. Another company official that responded to our survey stated that the audit market was an oligopoly with little price competition and too little concern for service. The CFO for another company commented on our survey that something needed to be done to force more competition, while a different CFO commented that although more competition was desirable, action to break up the largest firms was not warranted.

Based on the results of our survey, 57 percent of public companies thought that the level of competition for audit services for their company was sufficient.

However, while about 70 percent of small companies saw the level of competition as adequate, only about 40 percent of large Fortune 1000 companies shared this view (figure 7). About half of midsize companies saw the level of competition as adequate.

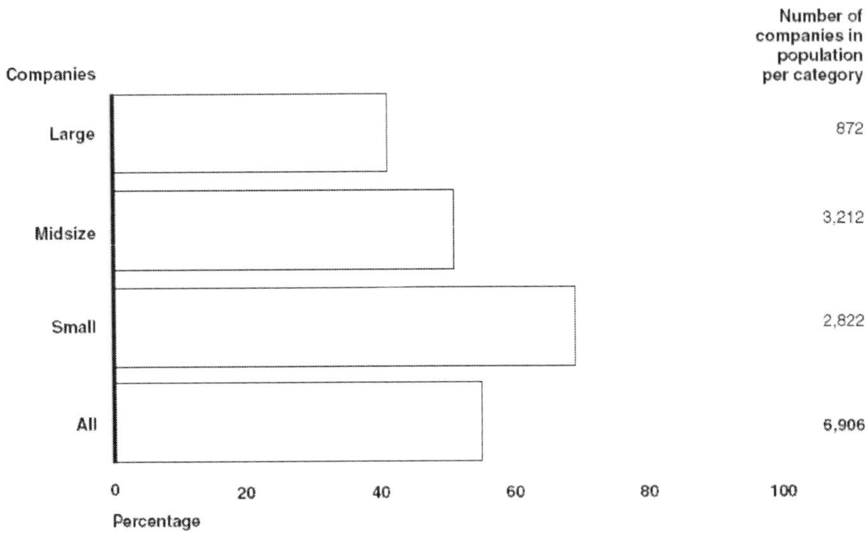

Source: GAO.

Note: Of the 6,906 companies in our survey population, 12.6 percent were large, 46.5 percent were midsize, and 40.9 percent were small.

Figure 7. Percentage of Public Companies Indicating That the Level of Audit Market Competition Was Sufficient.

Factors Increasing Audit Fees

Although highly concentrated markets typically raise concerns about price competition, our analysis indicated that other factors appeared to explain the increases in audit fees in recent years. Data on audit fees paid by public companies show that these fees have increased substantially since 2000, a period that included the dissolution of Arthur Andersen and the passage of the Sarbanes-Oxley Act. Audit fees have risen for companies of all sizes and across industries and regions. However, the fee increases, as a percentage of client company assets, were most dramatic for smaller companies. Between 2000 and 2006, median fees as a percent of assets more than quadrupled (a 334 percent increase) for companies with less than $100 million in revenue, more than tripled (a 239 percent increase) for companies with revenue between $100 million and $1 billion, and almost tripled (a 190 percent increase) for companies with revenue over $1 billion. After these increases, median fees were about $111,000 for companies with less than $100 million in revenue, $900,000 for companies with revenue between $100 million and $1 billion, and $3,156,000 for companies with revenue greater than $1 billion. Although audit fees increased significantly on average for all sizes of firms, the amount that companies spend on audit fees generally remains a small portion of their overall revenues.

Market participants and others cited various factors that had contributed to recent fee increases. The most significant factors that staff from the largest firms cited in interviews were the increasing complexity of accounting and financial reporting standards and the additional requirements of new auditing standards that had increased the amount of work involved in audits and the need for technical expertise. For example, one of the largest firms noted that the number of experts on staff at the firm more than doubled between 2003 and 2007. Many market participants noted similar factors as impacting fees. The largest firms also cited the increased costs of attracting and retaining talented staff and specialists. Similarly, midsize and smaller firms reported on our survey that the top four factors increasing their costs since 2003 were complexity of accounting principles and auditing standards, additional requirements of new standards, the time and effort necessary to prepare for PCAOB inspections, and the costs incurred to hire and train staff.

In particular, the Sarbanes-Oxley Act, which increased the amount of audit work performed at public companies, was frequently cited as one of the major factors in the recent fee increases. This legislation introduced a number of new requirements for audits of public companies, and many market participants told us that the new requirements accounted for much of the fee increases since 2002. Representatives from some audit firms we spoke to said that section 404 of the act had, where implemented, substantially increased their workload and costs for implementing new methodologies and staff training. (Section 404 requires the accounting firm to attest to, and report on, management's assessment of the effectiveness of its internal control over financial reporting.) In addition, 84 percent of companies reporting that their audit fees had increased since 2003 indicated on our survey that the audit of internal control over financial reporting was one of the reasons for the increase. To date, only larger public companies—which SEC calls accelerated filers—have had to comply with the new requirements for assessing these internal controls. Smaller public companies—those considered nonaccelerated filers—are scheduled to fully comply with the new audit requirements in annual filings after December 15, 2008, potentially resulting in further increases in these companies' audit fees.

Independence requirements may also have changed the way some firms price audits, resulting in rising fees. DOJ officials and others stated that audit firms were now less likely to price audits as a loss leader in order to sell nonaudit services because of these requirements in the Sarbanes-Oxley Act.

Effects of Concentration on Fee Increases

The results of an econometric model we developed to assess the extent to which various factors could be influencing audit fees in recent years also indicated that factors other than concentration appear to explain audit fees.[35] Our model analyzes the extent to which audit fees paid by public companies appear to be explained by a variety of factors that could affect those fees. For example, our model included such variables as the concentration within the audit market for a particular industry (as measured by HHI), the size of the company, whether the company's fiscal year ends during a busy period, whether the company completed a Sarbanes-Oxley Section 404 internal control audit, the number of times the company changed auditors, and other factors that could affect the company's audit fees. Appendix V explains our model in detail.

The results of our model suggested that higher audit market concentration across individual industries was not associated with higher audit fees. Specifically, our model found that, in general, public companies operating in industrial sectors with more concentrated audit markets were not paying higher audit fees than companies in sectors with less concentrated audit markets. However, for the largest companies we found some evidence that audit market concentration within an industry did have a very small effect on fees.[36] More precisely, after isolating the effect of other factors, our model results indicated that large companies in industries with audit markets that were 10 percent more concentrated than the average industry sector (as measured by HHI) paid on average about half a percent more in audit fees than other large companies. By comparison, the model results also indicated, after controlling for other factors, that companies that completed the Sarbanes-Oxley section 404 internal control audit, which increased the amount of work done by auditors, paid roughly 45 percent more in audit fees than companies that did not complete the internal control audit. This finding was consistent with estimates from other studies that examined the effect of the implementation of this requirement. Although factors other than concentration appeared to explain audit fee levels, the available data did not allow us to conclude that audit fees were competitive overall or to determine whether individual companies were charged competitive fees.[37]

In addition, the analysis we conducted with our model indicated that individual accounting firms appeared to charge higher fees when they controlled a large portion of the audit market within a particular industry, but this finding did not appear to be the result of anticompetitive pricing. Rather, it appeared that these firms may have been charging a premium for their industry expertise. We found that the price premiums received by accounting firms that collected a large share of the revenues from audits conducted within an industry sector were similar across all sizes of companies, including those small companies that typically have many accounting firms to choose from. This suggests that higher fees are more likely the result of these firms being able to charge premiums as the result of their industry expertise rather than of anticompetitive pricing.[38] For example, a firm with industry expertise may develop and market audit services that are specific to clients in the industry and that provide a level of service exceeding that provided by other firms in the same industry. If this is the case, the higher fees these firms may charge could reflect the specialized service they offer rather than anticompetitive pricing.

Other Potential Effects of Concentration

While some market participants expressed concern that concentration in the audit market could negatively affect audit quality, others said that the quality of audits had improved in recent years. According to DOJ and FTC guidance on analyzing market competitiveness, sellers with market power may lessen competition on dimensions other than price, such as product quality, service, or innovation. However, even in highly concentrated markets, including oligopolies, competition among sellers may lead to innovation and high-quality products. The effect of concentration on audit quality is difficult to measure empirically. However, we asked market participants about their views on several aspects of audit quality, including the experience and technical capability of their accounting firm's partners and staff, the firm's ability to efficiently respond to client needs, and its ability and willingness to appropriately identify and surface material reporting issues in financial reports. Most market participants who commented on audit quality in our interviews and many on our survey said that audit quality had improved, which some attributed to the Sarbanes-Oxley Act.[39] However, four others, including some academics, a former regulatory official, and an industry consultant with whom we spoke, expressed concerns that concentration was affecting the quality of audits. For example, one said that that having only four firms in the market resulted in low-quality audits that harmed investors. Appendix IV provides more information on trends in audit costs and quality.

High concentration may also diminish competition because dominant sellers, in this case accounting firms, may be more likely or more able to engage in coordinated interaction in ways that can affect auditing practices or prices. Some market participants we interviewed expressed concern that the prevalence of the largest firms on advisory panels or standard-setting bodies enabled them to coordinate actions to influence the development of new standards in a way that hampered competition or otherwise disadvantaged public company audit clients. However, most market participants we spoke to did not express such concerns.

FURTHER CONCENTRATION COULD ADVERSELY AFFECT AUDIT FEES AND LIMIT CHOICES

Although the current level of concentration does not appear to be having significant adverse effect, the potential for further concentration in the audit market did raise concerns. Further concentration could arise as a result of several events. For example, audit firms face the risk that civil litigation could result in their insolvency or inability to continue operations. Since 1998, audit firms may have paid at least ten settlements or awards of $100 million or more that have resulted from private litigation.[40] In addition, a jury recently found BDO Seidman, the sixth-largest accounting firm, liable for $521.7 million in damages, although BDO Seidman plans to appeal the verdict. Several officials we spoke with commented that litigation increases during periods of high market volatility. As a result, litigation-related costs to auditors could increase in the case of an economic downturn. Officials from the largest firms told us that litigation costs have significantly increased since 2003. Some officials we interviewed from the largest firms and the insurance industry told us that the largest firms do not have insurance coverage to protect against the largest claims, both because insurance at that level is not available and because of fear that having more insurance could induce plaintiffs to seek higher awards. However, full information on litigation risk and costs and accounting firms' insurance coverage is not publicly available, so we could not identify the magnitude of the risk that litigation poses to these firms. Some officials we spoke with also suggested that litigation could damage a firm's reputation, causing the firm to fail if its clients began seeking other firms for their audits. For example, according to some academics, Laventhol and

Horwath, the seventh-largest accounting firm in 1990, declared bankruptcy that year in part due to a series of class action lawsuits that resulted in a loss of reputation and the firm's inability to attract new work.[41]

Firms also face the risk of failure from federal or state regulatory action and criminal prosecution, among other reasons. State Boards of Accountancy can revoke accounting firms' licenses to practice in their state for violating board rules or for other reasons. Under SEC rules, convicted felons shall be suspended from practicing before the SEC, so an accounting firm convicted of a felony could not continue to audit its SEC-registered clients and would likely fail. Further, an indictment for a felony could contribute to a firm's failure if clients began leaving in anticipation of a potential conviction. For example, many of Arthur Andersen's clients had changed to a different auditor even before Arthur Andersen was convicted of obstruction of justice for destroying Enron-related documents in 2002. The market for public company audits could also become significantly more concentrated if any of the existing largest or midsize firms chose to discontinue operations for other reasons. Mismanagement of a firm's financial obligations could also lead to its bankruptcy.

As has happened in the past, a merger could also lead to further concentration in the market. DOJ and the Federal Trade Commission published Horizontal Merger Guidelines for use in determining whether a merger is likely substantially to lessen competition. The guidelines include steps for assessing whether the merger would significantly increase concentration, the potential for any of the firms to exercise market power after the merger, and the difficulty of entry into the market for new firms. Concerns that DOJ raised about a proposed merger of accounting firms in the late 1990s suggest that the agency would be less likely to approve any future mergers among the largest accounting firms. In 1997, shortly after two of the six largest firms at the time, PriceWaterhouse and Coopers and Lybrand, announced their intention to merge, two of the other six largest firms, KPMG Peat Marwick and Ernst and Young, also announced plans to combine their operations. According to the DOJ Antitrust Division's 1999 Annual Report, these two firms abandoned their plans to merge after DOJ raised concerns that this merger would have "adversely affected competition by reducing the already limited number of firms providing auditing services to Fortune 1000 companies."[42]

The loss of another large accounting firm from the audit market could significantly increase the level of concentration. If one of the largest firms failed or left the market, concentration would increase if many of this firm's public company clients engaged one of the remaining three largest audit firms. To illustrate the effect of such an event, we simulated the effect of the failure or exit of the smallest of the largest firms. To redistribute the clients of this firm, we assigned them to other firms in the same proportion as the clients of Arthur Andersen were distributed after that firm dissolved.[43] Under this scenario, the resulting HHI of the overall audit market would rise from 2,300 to roughly 3,000, substantially above what DOJ considers to be a highly concentrated market. The increase in HHI would likely be even greater in the large public company market. Higher concentration could increase the risk that the remaining large accounting firms would exercise market power to raise prices and coordinate their actions among themselves to the detriment of their clients. Appendix II contains more information on our simulations of the result of the loss of one of the largest firms through a failure or a merger.

Further concentration could have various other negative effects on public companies and their investors. While many public companies and other market participants indicated that there were enough auditors to choose from, further concentration would leave large companies with potentially only one or two choices for a new auditor, as our survey indicated that 86 percent of large companies would likely only use one of the largest auditors if they had to switch auditors. Many interviewees said that this would not be enough choices. As in the current market, independence rules that prevent companies from using as their auditor firms that provide them with certain nonaudit services could further limit these choices. Also, companies in specialized industries could have fewer choices if some accounting firms do not operate in those industries. Many we interviewed also suggested that further concentration would reduce competition and potentially increase the cost of an audit.

Further, public company officials stated that changing auditors could be costly for the companies involved. According to our survey results, 44 percent of large companies that had not recently changed auditors reported that the burdens of time, effort, and cost were of great or very great importance in their decision not to change auditors. In addition, only 102 large (Fortune 1000) public company auditor changes occurred between January 2003 and June 2007, suggesting that large companies preferred to use the same auditor from year to year. If the market were further concentrated among three large firms, the affected companies would need to change auditors and incur the associated costs. Similarly, to the extent the remaining largest firms resigned as auditors for smaller clients as they absorbed the failed firm's larger clients, these small companies would incur the costs of finding a new auditor. Finally, the market disruption caused by a firm failure or exit from the market could affect companies' abilities to obtain timely audits of their financial statements, reducing the audited financial information available to investors.

REGULATORS COULD ACT TO MITIGATE THE EFFECTS OF FURTHER CONCENTRATION

If the number of large accounting firms were to decrease, the organizations with oversight responsibility for the public company audit market could act to mitigate the effects on the market. The organizations that have a role in overseeing aspects of the public company audit market include SEC, PCAOB, and DOJ. SEC is responsible for protecting investors, maintaining efficient markets, and facilitating capital formation and also oversees PCAOB. Similarly, PCAOB is responsible for overseeing the auditors of public companies in order to protect the interests of investors and further the public interest in the preparation of informative, fair, and independent audit reports. In the event of the loss of one of the largest firms, the agencies' actions could vary according to the facts and circumstances of the situation, such as the size of the affected firm, the reason the firm left the market, or the degree to which an orderly transition of audit services was available. For example, in order to support its mission and address temporary market disruptions and difficulties companies had in meeting financial reporting deadlines when Arthur Andersen was indicted in 2002, SEC issued a number of measures providing guidance and regulatory relief to Arthur Andersen's clients. This rulemaking provided Arthur Andersen clients with extended deadlines to submit audited financial statements and hotline numbers for companies and investors to call with questions.[44] Through the International Organization of Securities Commissions (IOSCO), SEC is also working with other securities regulators around the world to identify possible actions regulators could consider in responding to events affecting the availability of audit services and to develop information for regulators to consider in contingency planning and crisis management.

Although it does not have a direct role in addressing the loss of a large accounting firm from the market, DOJ would have a role in reviewing proposed mergers involving accounting firms. As part of ensuring competition in the U.S. economy, the Antitrust Division of DOJ is responsible for enforcing antitrust laws. Under DOJ merger guidelines, the division would challenge any merger likely to substantially lessen competition. DOJ officials explained that action on their part would only occur if a merger among current competitors was proposed or if an antitrust or criminal case was brought against one of the firms. As a result, the division has not been formally reviewing trends in the market. When asked whether the Antitrust Division might review the competitiveness of the market if one of the largest firms exited the market for reasons other than a merger, an official stated that the division might analyze the market using publicly available information and offer its expertise and advice to other regulators. However, the division does not have the authority to formally investigate the market or request proprietary information from firms or companies in such a situation.

Chapter 4

Midsize and Smaller Firms Face Challenges Auditing Public Companies, and Growth in These Firms Is Unlikely to Ease Concentration in the Large Public Company Audit Market

Growth in the capacity of midsize and smaller audit firms is unlikely to reduce concentration in the large company audit market, at least in the near term, for two reasons. First, our survey and interviews with representatives of these firms suggest that over 70 percent of midsize and smaller firms are not interested in expanding their market share by adding additional large public company audit clients because they would face additional risks and give up existing profitable activities to do so. Second, firms that do want to audit large public companies continue to face challenges to expanding their public company practices. Chief among these challenges are having adequate capacity (e.g., staff and geographic coverage) to audit large public companies, acquiring the needed technical capability and industry specialization, and developing name recognition and a reputation for this kind of work. Similar challenges also affect midsize and smaller firms that audit small and midsize public companies. Some firms are taking actions to reduce certain challenges, such as increasing their geographic reach by joining networks and affiliations. But many firms and market participants we interviewed also said that the growth of smaller firms was unlikely to ease concentration in the market for auditors of large public companies.

Midsize and Smaller Firms Face Several Disincentives and Challenges to Entering the Large Public Company Audit Market

While most midsize and smaller audit firms expect to grow in the next five years, only a small number want to enter or expand their share of the large company audit market, in part because they would face additional risks and forego currently profitable nonaudit activities to do so. According to our survey of the 118 accounting firms with at least 5 public company clients, the 4 midsize firms and 79 percent of the smaller firms that responded expected to increase the number of public companies they audited in the next 5 years.[45] However, when asked if they would consider expanding their market share if they had the opportunity to add acceptable clients, 74 percent of both midsize and smaller firms said that they were not interested in serving as auditor for additional large public companies.[46] Some firms and market participants told us that the possibility of being sued created a disincentive against entering or expanding in the audit market for large companies because the failure of one large client could jeopardize the audit firm. Large companies can pose a greater financial risk to their auditors than smaller clients. The amount shareholders recovered in settlements of class action lawsuits against public companies and their auditors tends to increase in proportion to the company's market capitalization. Midsize and smaller firms also may not be seeking to perform audits of large public companies, because they have had new opportunities to provide companies of all sizes with nonaudit services, such as consulting, since 2003. The Sarbanes-Oxley Act's independence standards prohibit firms from providing clients whose financial statements they audit with some of the nonaudit services that they were accustomed to providing. As a result, many smaller firms have moved into this area. However, 21 percent of midsize and smaller firms said that they would be willing to enter or expand their share of market for auditing large companies, given the opportunity and acceptable potential clients, but emphasized the challenges they faced in doing so.

Firm Capacity to Audit Larger Companies

According to midsize and smaller firms responding to our survey, their capacity to audit large public companies poses the greatest challenge to them entering this market and reducing its concentration. According to our survey, the firms' capacity is the top reason that large public companies give to explain why they would not consider using a midsize or smaller firm. Specifically, 92 percent of those companies said that the inability of midsize and smaller firms to handle their company's size and complexity was of great or very great importance in their unwillingness to consider them (figure 8).[47] For example, the audit committee chairman of a large technology manufacturing company we interviewed said that an auditor smaller than the company's current large firm could not audit a business of his company's size. Similarly, the audit committee chair for a large automobile manufacturer told us that large companies did not consider using midsize firms because those firms did not have the number of experienced staff that the firms had.

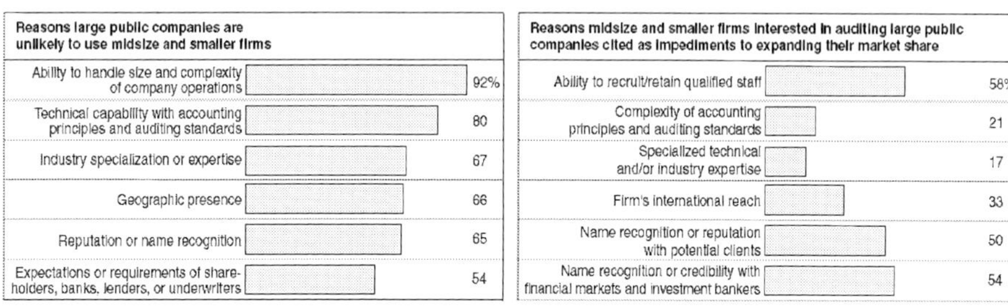

Source: GAO.

Figure 8. Firms' Challenges in Auditing Large Public Companies.

To meaningfully reduce concentration in the large public company market, then, midsize and smaller firms would need to staff audit teams that were large enough to serve multiple large public companies. However, these firms face challenges recruiting and retaining staff. As we reported in 2003, it is not uncommon for an audit of a large national or multinational public company to require hundreds of staff, and most midsize and smaller firms do not have the staff resources necessary to commit hundreds of employees to a single client. As table 2 illustrates, the largest firms have significantly more capacity, in terms of staff and partners than midsize and smaller firms.

Table 2. Largest, Midsize, and Smaller Accounting Firm Capacity, 2006

Firm	Partners[a]	Professional staff[b]	Offices	Public company clients
Largest				
Deloitte and Touche LLP	2,654	26,960	98	1,377
Ernst and Young LLP	2,100	17,200	83	1,743
PricewaterhouseCoopers LLP	2,069	21,409	84	1,347
KPMG LLP	1,664	14,038	89	1,210
Midsize				
McGladrey and Pullen LLP[c]	775	4,567	125	103
Grant Thornton LLP	444	3,575	48	411
BDO Seidman LLP	240	1,803	34	301
Crowe Chizek and Company	129	1,458	20	104
Smaller[d]				
Average of sample of smaller firms	46	332	8	20

Source: Public Accounting Report, 2006-2007.

[a] Equity partners, including those who do not work on audits.

[b] Nonequity partners and professionals.

[c] RSM McGladrey and McGladrey and Pullen are affiliated through an alternative practice structure. The number of offices includes those for RSM McGladrey, which is a subsidiary of H and R Block and performs tax and consulting services and for McGladrey and Pullen, which performs audit services.

[d] Sample of smaller firms that audit at least one public company.

To approach the capacity of the largest firms, midsize and smaller firms would have to grow substantially. The gap between the largest and midsize firms is significant, however. Combined, the four midsize firms still have over 2,600 fewer professional staff than the smallest of the largest firms, KPMG. The midsize firms also have significantly fewer public company clients. But midsize and smaller firms told us that obtaining additional staff to expand their audit practices was difficult. Specifically, 58 percent of midsize and smaller firms responding to our survey that want to audit large public companies said that the ability to recruit and retain qualified staff was a great or very great impediment to expansion. While the representatives from the largest firms told us that they also faced this challenge, one smaller firm representative said obtaining sufficient numbers of staff was particularly difficult for smaller firms, which have fewer resources (salaries and benefits) to use in competing for talent with the largest firms, the public companies themselves, and others needing public accountants. According to many market participants we interviewed, the demand for qualified accountants has increased significantly in recent years because accounting firms, including the largest firms, need additional staff to conduct the audits of internal controls required in section 404 of the Sarbanes-Oxley Act. Firms are not only competing with each other for staff, but also with public companies that need additional accounting staff to comply with certain requirements of Sarbanes-Oxley. In addition, firms are competing with regulators who need more staff to oversee the accounting profession. In the face of this increased demand, hiring such staff has become more expensive.

Constraints on midsize and smaller firms' geographic reach also reduced the likelihood that the growth of these firms will reduce concentration in the large company market. As table 2 shows, midsize and smaller firms generally have fewer offices than the largest firms. Accounting firm representatives also told us that these firms have a smaller presence in foreign countries than the largest firms. According to our survey, 66 percent of large companies that would not consider using a midsize or smaller firm said that these firms' geographic presence was of great or very great importance in explaining their unwillingness to do so. Large multinational companies in particular need auditors that have a presence in all of the countries in which they operate. While many midsize and smaller firms partner with other independent firms to expand their geographic reach, a few company officials we interviewed said that most of the international networks these firms belong to are not extensive enough to meet their companies' needs. In addition, many market participants we interviewed were concerned that the quality standards, practices, and internal controls of these networks and affiliations might be less uniform than those prevailing in the international networks of the largest firms.

Accounting firm representatives we interviewed had mixed views on the global capabilities of midsize and smaller firms. In spite of companies' views on the importance of firms' abilities to provide global services, only one-third of midsize and smaller firms responding to our survey that want to audit large public companies said that their firms' international reach was a great or very great impediment to expansion. For example, one accounting firm official told us that midsize firms and affiliations had good global capabilities and global operations. However, another accounting firm official told us that the global networks used by midsize and smaller firms needed to add standardized quality controls in order to improve.

Technical Capability and Industry Specialization

The technical capabilities and specialized industry knowledge of midsize and smaller firms that want to enter the large public company market can also limit these firms' ability to enter this market and reduce its concentration. According to our survey, 80 percent of large public companies that would not consider using a midsize or smaller firm said that such firms' technical capabilities with accounting principles and auditing standards was a great or very great reason why they would not do so. One official from a large public company whom we interviewed said that accounting firms' technical capabilities differentiate the largest and smaller firms and that smaller firms did not have the resources to keep up with changing auditing standards and increasingly complex accounting rules around the world. Other company officials we interviewed also said that technical capabilities were an important reason why large and complex companies do not use midsize and smaller firms.

Several representatives of smaller accounting firms also told us that their firms had difficulty maintaining their technical capabilities. For example, one representative of a smaller firm noted that his firm had less depth in terms of technical expertise than larger firms especially when it came to complex transactions. Other firms said that maintaining technical expertise was time-consuming and costly. Two representatives of smaller firms noted that keeping up with new standards and guidance from multiple sources was also difficult, requiring the firms to revise guidance for their staff as new standards were implemented or to purchase costly prepared guidance materials from external sources. However, firms see this as less of an issue than do their clients. Only 21 percent of accounting firms responding to our survey that want to audit large companies said that the complexity of accounting principles and auditing standards were a great or very great impediment to expansion, compared to 80 percent of clients.

In addition, having sufficient industry expertise can be challenging for firms that want to audit large public companies. According to our survey, 67 percent of large public companies that would not consider using midsize and smaller firms said that such firms' industry specialization or expertise was of great or very great importance in their unwillingness to do so. Some large public companies told us that they needed this kind of industry expertise in their auditor. For example, the audit committee chairman for a large insurance company told us that when he chooses an audit firm, industry expertise was the most important factor he considered. He said that his company's audit firm must have experience with other companies in the insurance industry and doubted that midsize or smaller firms could meet these requirements.

Several representatives of smaller accounting firms whom we interviewed said that industry expertise was a significant barrier to auditing large public companies. For instance, a representative of one smaller accounting firm noted that before accepting a new client, her firm was very careful to ensure that it has the right expertise to do the audit. She said that since the firm's expertise was in distribution and manufacturing, the firm would not accept a financial institution client. An official from another midsize firm told us that industry specialization was important because audits were not commodities. Instead, these accounting firms specialized in certain industries and had particular areas of expertise. This emphasis on industry expertise can limit midsize and smaller firms' ability to expand their businesses to serve companies that operate in industries outside of their specialty. However, only 17 percent of accounting firms responding to our survey that want to audit large companies said that specialized technical or industry expertise was a great or very great impediment to expansion.

Accounting Firm Reputation

Another major barrier to midsize and smaller firms' ability to obtain large company clients is that these auditors do not have the reputations the largest firms enjoy. According to our survey, 65 percent of large companies that would not consider using a midsize or smaller firm said that reputation or name recognition were great or very great reasons that they were unwilling to do so. In addition, company officials told us that they were confident that the largest firms could meet their companies' audit needs because these auditors had well-established reputations for quality. These officials were less familiar with the smaller firms' work and thus were uncertain about the ability of such a firm to adequately serve their companies. Market participants told us that conducting due diligence on unfamiliar firms was time-consuming, in part because information was not readily available. Furthermore, although PCAOB has begun inspecting accounting firms' audit work, many market participants we interviewed said that the information currently available from the PCAOB inspection reports was not sufficient to judge a firm's audit capabilities. For example, some noted that part of the inspection results were not published, inspection reports were not always timely, and PCAOB did not make an overall judgment on a firm's quality.[48]

Companies are also responding to their perceptions of investors' preferences when they choose one of the largest auditors. According to our survey, 54 percent of large companies that would not consider using a midsize or smaller firm said that the expectations or requirements of shareholders, banks, lenders, or the underwriters that help the company raise capital were of great or very great importance in their unwillingness to do so. Institutional investors and investment banks often use a company's financial statements and audits as the starting point in an investment decision and want to have confidence in the auditor that reviewed the financial statements. Similarly, representatives from an investment bank and an institutional investor told us that they preferred auditors with established reputations because of a lack of familiarity with capabilities of most midsize and smaller firms. One company official we interviewed said that she did not know why a larger company would not want to use one of the largest firms, given that these firms' name recognition provided underwriters with a certain comfort level. In addition, investment bank representatives told us that they want companies to use auditors with sufficient financial resources to withstand a liability judgment against them. For example, if an investment deal falters, the investment bank or underwriter may have to assume more of the settlement costs if the audit firm cannot bear its share. Furthermore, one investor told us that the largest firms' greater financial resources made them better able to survive a large client's failure.

Midsize and smaller firms agree that name recognition and reputation pose a challenge to entering the audit market for large companies. Fifty percent of accounting firms responding to our survey that want to audit large companies said that name recognition or reputation with potential clients was a great or very great impediment to expansion. Similarly, 54 percent of these firms cited name recognition or credibility with financial markets and investment bankers as a great or very great impediment to expansion. In addition, some accounting firm representatives we interviewed said that midsize and smaller firms have had fewer opportunities to compete with the largest firms for large companies' business and do not have well-established reputations. However, one midsize firm representative noted that reputation should become less of an impediment as more companies moved from the largest firms to smaller firms and these firms' work became better known.

An analysis of data on firms that audit initial public offerings (IPOs) illustrates investors' preferences for the largest firms in certain situations. While midsize and smaller firms' combined share of the IPO market has grown progressively, rising from 18 percent to 40 percent since 2003, the largest firms have consistently audited the majority of IPOs (figure 9). Staff from some investment firms that underwrite stock issuances for public companies told us that in the past they generally had expected the companies for which they raised capital to use one of the largest firms for IPOs but that now these organizations were more willing to accept smaller audit firms. For example, an official from one investment firm told us that the firm now generally accepted two of the midsize audit firms for IPOs or securities issuances. However, as figure 9 shows, most of the companies that went public with a midsize or smaller auditor were smaller. In addition, these firms' share of IPOs of larger companies (those with revenues greater than $150 million) rose from none in 2003 to about 13 percent in 2007.

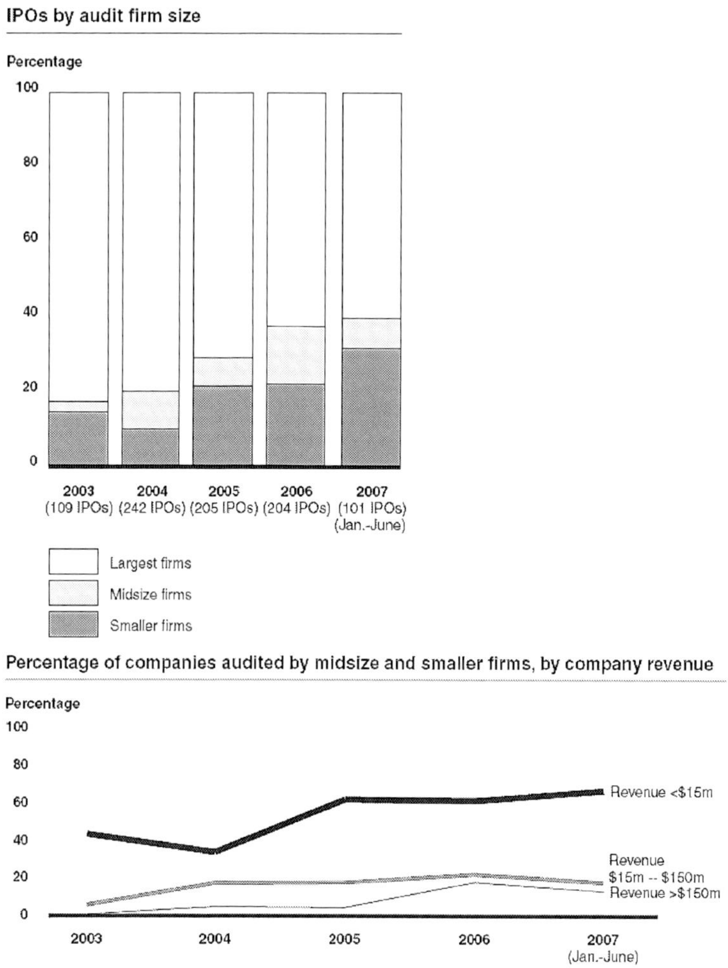

Note: Changes in the business environment and audit market during this period make judgments based on year-to-year comparisons difficult.

Figure 9. IPOs, 2003-2007.

Midsize and smaller firms responding to our survey indicated that they had had mixed experiences assisting clients with IPOs. All of the midsize firms and 82 percent of smaller firms responding to our survey had assisted new and existing clients with an IPO or subsequent securities issuance. However, two of the four midsize firms, as well as 36 percent of the smaller firms, reported losing clients that wanted another firm, often one of the largest firms, to help them prepare for an IPO or subsequent securities issuance.

Similar Challenges Affect Midsize and Smaller Accounting Firms in the Market for Small and Midsize Companies

Midsize and smaller accounting firms responding to our survey said that they faced challenges even in competing in the market for smaller public company audits. Our survey respondents in this market generally reported that the challenges they faced were significant impediments to increasing the number of public companies they served. As shown in figure 10, these challenges, such as firms' capacity, global reach, and technical capability or expertise, are similar to those facing midsize and smaller firms that want to audit large companies.

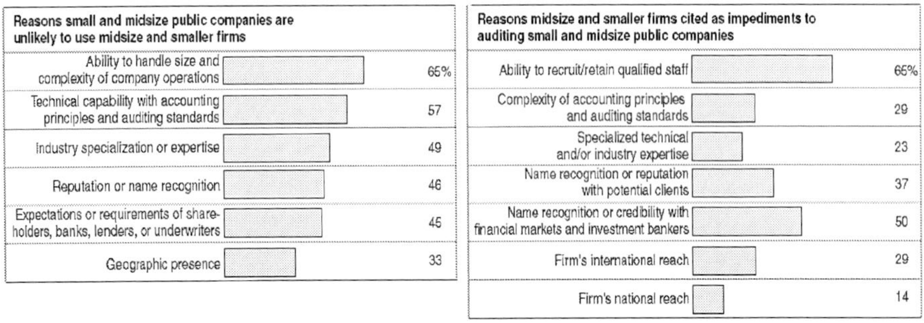

Figure 10. Midsize and Smaller Firms' Challenges in Auditing Small and Midsize Companies.

To increase their capacity and geographic reach, accounting firms need the financial capital to hire new staff or acquire other audit firms, but capital constraints and expansion costs pose an impediment to growth for some midsize and smaller firms. While this constraint could affect firms of all sizes, midsize and smaller firms have fewer partners from whom they can obtain capital. Of the midsize and smaller firms responding to our survey that focus on smaller companies, 65 percent said that the costs of hiring and training additional staff were a great or very great impediment to expansion. According to an accounting firm representative we interviewed, some smaller firms can be constrained from raising capital to expand their businesses because of the partnership structure, which requires individual partners to pool their own assets or assume debt for acquisitions and other growth activities, such as hiring new staff. However, one midsize firm representative said that raising capital for expansion was not an impediment for his firm.

Smaller firms responding to our survey also told us that complying with the many different requirements individual states impose could hinder their efforts to audit clients with operations in multiple states. Each of the 50 states and 5 U.S. territories have state boards of accountancy that have sole authority for establishing licensing requirements for certified public accountants in their jurisdictions. If a company's business operations extend across state lines, auditors may need to get temporary certifications in each of the states where they will conduct audit work. These requirements can range in complexity and cost among the several states. Some firms we interviewed said that complying with multiple state licensing requirements was difficult and often expensive. However, only 27 percent of midsize and smaller firms responding to our survey that focus on smaller companies said that varied state licensing requirements were great or very great impediments to expansion. Furthermore, some representatives of accounting firms whom we interviewed said that multiple state requirements did not stop them from competing for new clients.

Smaller Audit Firms Are Taking Actions to Expand Their Market Share, but Challenges Remain

Many midsize and smaller firms have taken steps to reduce the challenges that they face and have successfully expanded their share of the audit market for small and midsize companies somewhat in recent years. In some cases, these firms have expanded their audit practices in niches that allow them to use their expertise, rather than attempting to serve clients in new industries. Some midsize and smaller firms told us that, while having staff with a certain type of expertise could be a barrier in trying to serve all types of companies, it did not hinder them if they focused on a more select set of industries. They said that this approach had allowed them to build their reputations in specialty areas, which may enable them to acquire progressively larger clients, and grow incrementally. Other firms told us that they had expanded their practices through mergers and acquisitions, adding new industry expertise, increasing their capacity, and extending their geographic reach. Smaller firms that responded to our survey generally viewed this approach as effective for increasing the number of companies they audited, with 73 percent saying that it was at least somewhat effective. Some representatives of midsize firms whom we interviewed also said that acquisitions were an effective way to expand into regions where they did not already have an office.

While funding for expanding midsize and smaller accounting firms typically came from loans from financial institutions, merging with other accounting firms, or the personal resources of the firm's partners, a small number of firms are using a different method of increasing their access to capital. These firms have established alternative practice structures, in which the firm engaged in attest services is closely aligned with another organization that performs other nonaudit services. One example is where owners of the accounting firm sell the nonaudit portion of their practice to a new entity, which may be publicly or privately owned. The work the firm previously conducted is then essentially divided into two separately controlled entities, one of which conducts most of the firm's nonaudit and attest work, while the other conducts audits. Owners of the audit firm are also employees of the nonaudit entity, and the audit firm generally leases employees, office space, equipment, administrative support, and other services from this entity. Audit firms gain additional access to capital from the initial sale of the nonaudit entity or loans from the new entity that they can use for acquisitions and other growth activities. However, some firms with alternative practice structures told us that getting approval for their organizations from some states was challenging and that they were subject to additional scrutiny because their uncommon structure raised concerns about independence.[49] In addition, 63 percent of midsize and smaller firms responding to our survey said that alternative practice structures would only be slightly or not at all effective in helping them increase their market share.

Finally, according to representatives of two accounting firm networks and affiliations of independent firms, these organizations help midsize and smaller firms deal with some of the challenges they face. As we have seen, some midsize and smaller firms join these networks in order to extend their geographic reach. In two cases that we reviewed, we found that the structure of these organizations varies widely. One organization was described as having a focused mission and high standards that member firms must continuously meet, while a representative from another said that the organization functioned primarily as a vehicle to share best practices and refer business to other member firms. All midsize firms and over 60 percent of smaller firms responding to our survey belonged to a network or affiliation, generally to increase competitiveness with larger firms and extend their national and international reach. One network representative we spoke to told us that the network's main benefit was its ability to serve clients that were expanding, especially internationally, by partnering with other firms in the network. In interviews, officials from two smaller firms also told us that networks and affiliations provided opportunities to serve new clients either by partnering with other firms or through referral services.

Midsize and smaller firms that responded to our survey had mixed views about the ability of these networks and affiliations to help increase their market share. Some market participants thought that networks' value could be limited because, unlike the global networks of the largest firms, the member firms of these networks and affiliations did not share a common set of methodologies or internal controls. In general, the firms in networks wanted to maintain their individuality in order to avoid being held liable for another firm's audit work. In addition, officials from two smaller firms that are members of a network expressed concern that the proposed independence standards of the International Federation of Accountants—the global organization for the accounting profession that develops international standards on ethics, auditing and assurance, education, and public sector accounting standards—could present additional challenges for networks because of the broad way that the standards define networks.[50] Officials with the International Federation of Accountants told us that the standards were still under consideration and that comments and concerns from accounting firms on this issue were still under review.

While the practices discussed above have helped smaller accounting firms to reduce some of the challenges they face, certain barriers are likely to persist, particularly in the market for large company audits. While focusing on niche markets can deepen a firm's expertise, just as mergers, acquisitions, and networks can increase firms' capacity and geographic reach, midsize and smaller firms are still much smaller than their large firm competitors and have much less experience in the large company audit market. Some market participants think that building up smaller firms' capacity, experience, and reputation to serve large companies is likely to be a long-term process, thus their growth is unlikely to ease concentration.

Chapter 5

Proposals for Addressing Concentration and Increasing Market Share for Smaller Auditors Have Significant Disadvantages

Over the years, academics, industry groups, and other market participants have offered a range of proposals that are intended to reduce the risks of current and further concentration, or address the expansion challenges facing midsize and smaller audit firms. We considered a number of these proposals and found that, while each could offer certain benefits, each proposal also presents at least some significant disadvantages, and market participants generally saw these proposals as having limited effectiveness, feasibility, and benefit. Since the current level of concentration does not appear to be having significant adverse effect, and the proposals we reviewed were generally not seen as effective in addressing the risks of concentration or challenges facing smaller firms without serious drawbacks, we found no compelling need to take action.

Proposals Others Have Made for Reducing the Risks of the Current Level of Concentration Involve Trade-offs

Several proposals have been offered to reduce the risks of the current level of concentration, including mandatory audit firm rotation, audit firm financial statement disclosure, and breaking up the largest firms into more firms.

Mandatory Audit Firm Rotation

Some academic and industry sources have suggested that requiring public companies to periodically change auditors could reduce the current level of concentration. Such mandatory audit firm rotation would limit the period of years that an accounting firm could serve as the auditor for a particular public company. Our survey results show that companies often retain their auditors for long periods of time.[51] For example, according to our survey results, approximately 40 percent of public companies had used their current auditor for at least 5 years, and almost a quarter had used their current auditor for at least 10 years.[52] While generally proposed as a means of enhancing auditor independence by periodically bringing in a new auditor for a "fresh look" at a company's financial statements, mandatory rotation could potentially reduce concentration to the extent that it provided more opportunities for midsize and smaller firms to compete to provide audit services to public companies.

Although mandatory auditor rotation would increase opportunities to compete, it would not increase the number of viable competitors, and views on its effectiveness as a means of reducing concentration were mixed. For example, 44 percent of midsize and smaller firms responding to our survey stated that mandatory rotation would be at least a somewhat effective way for their firms to gain more public company clients, and 52 percent of respondents thought that it would be only slightly or not at all effective.[53] One person we interviewed noted that mandatory rotation might not be feasible, since some companies had very limited choices due in part to the restrictions of independence requirements. Another market participant noted that mandatory rotation would not necessarily reduce concentration because large public companies would likely just rotate to another one of the largest firms. In a 2003 report on the potential effects of mandatory audit firm rotation, we found similar results.[54] Based on surveys we conducted for that report, 83 percent of accounting firms that audit 10 or more companies and 66 percent of Fortune 1000 public companies stated that under mandatory auditor rotation, the market for public company audits would either become more concentrated or remain about the same. Further, more than half of accounting firms that audit 10 or more companies felt that mandatory audit firm rotation would reduce the number of firms willing and able to compete for public company audits.

In addition, market participants we spoke with raised other concerns about mandatory audit firm rotation. Some said that mandatory rotation would increase both audit firms' and public companies' costs. In our 2003 report, we found that many audit firms and large companies surveyed believed that mandatory rotation would increase initial year audit-related costs by more than 30 percent. For example, we reported that audit firms could incur higher marketing costs as they increased efforts to acquire or retain clients. With new auditors every few years, public companies also would incur higher support costs for assisting the new audit firm in understanding the companies' operations, systems, and financial reporting practices. Others expressed concern that new audit firms would need a period of time to become fully familiar with a client's operations. Lacking knowledge, and the time that would be required to acquire it, could increase the risk of an auditor not detecting financial reporting issues that could materially affect the company's financial statements.

Other recently implemented regulatory changes may have already provided at least one of the benefits this proposal is designed to provide. The Sarbanes-Oxley Act requires mandatory rotation of lead and reviewing audit partners after they have provided audit services to a particular public company for five consecutive years. Many market participants we interviewed for our 2003 report suggested that this requirement, when fully implemented, could achieve some of the independence benefits related to a new auditor's having a fresh look at a company's financial statements.[55]

Audit Firm Financial Statement Disclosure

Another proposal that has been offered would require public company auditors to provide financial information that could also be used to assess the competitiveness of audit fee levels. Some market participants and others advocate requiring accounting firms that audit public companies to disclose detailed financial information, such as their own revenues and profits. They have noted that providing this information could increase the transparency of the market and help participants evaluate its profitability, and the information could also help market regulators and others evaluate whether firms were charging prices above competitive levels.

Jurisdictions outside the United States have begun requiring audit firms to disclose some financial information, but the results have been unclear. In the United Kingdom, audit firms are required to file financial information. However, because U.K. accounting firms provide many services, some find the consolidated financial statement to be of limited usefulness in assessing the economics of the firms' audit services. As a result, based on the advice of a group of market participants, the U.K. Financial Reporting Council recommended that audit firms disclose the financial results of their work on statutory audits and directly related services, so that "clearer and more comparable information on the profitability of audit work" would be available.[56] In addition, beginning in 2008, audit firms that carry out statutory audits in the European Union are required to file information on fees charged for audits and other services, as well as data on the basis for partners' compensation.

Most market participants we interviewed on this proposal did not believe that requiring audit firms to publicly disclose their financial results would be very effective in reducing the risk of anticompetitive pricing among the largest accounting firms. Some market participants we spoke with indicated that such financial statements would not provide useful information for evaluating whether firms were charging fees above competitive levels. Others familiar with the accounting profession have commented that regulators already had the authority to request certain financial information from firms if needed. Therefore, this proposal might not have any direct effect on market competition.

Breaking up the Largest Firms into More Firms

Some academics and former regulators have suggested that requiring one or more of the largest firms to spin off a large portion of their operations to create more than four firms with the capacity to audit large public companies could ease current concentration. Breaking up the largest firms would at least temporarily decrease concentration and mitigate the adverse effect of one of the firms exiting the market or failing. Firms in other markets have been split up in the past—for example, Standard Oil and the American Tobacco Company in 1911; meatpacking firms in 1920; and AT and T, which owned all regional operating telephone companies, in 1984. In some of these cases, some of the resulting companies merged in later years after market or technological changes.

Market participants we spoke with expressed concerns about the potential adverse effects of forcing the largest firms to divest themselves of some of their operations. For example, several indicated that splitting the firms could entail significant costs and diminish the economies of scale and depth of expertise that currently allow the largest firms to audit large public companies with complex technical needs and worldwide operations. The result could be increased audit costs and decreased quality of audits performed. In the public company survey we conducted for our 2003 report on accounting firm consolidation we found that 79 percent of survey respondents opposed breaking up the largest firms.[57] Though a few we interviewed thought that this proposal would be effective in reducing concentration, those we interviewed on this topic generally agreed that it was not very feasible and that it could be complicated, difficult, and costly. These adverse results seem especially disruptive in the absence of compelling evidence that current levels of concentration were causing harm.

Reducing the Impact or Risk of Litigation Could Prevent Further Concentration, but Proposals to Achieve this Goal Have Been Questioned

The risk of being sued appears to reduce some audit firms' willingness to seek out additional public company clients. We reported in 2003 that litigation risk was a barrier for smaller firms seeking to audit larger public companies because of the difficulty of managing this risk and of obtaining affordable liability insurance.[58] In the survey we conducted for this report, over half (61 percent) of midsize and smaller audit firms reported that liability/tort reform would be at least somewhat effective in helping them increase their market share. Further, litigation could result in even more market concentration if firms that were sued ultimately went out of business. Several proposals have been made to reduce the potential for litigation to cause further concentration in the market for audit services, including placing caps on auditors' liability and targeting enforcement against responsible individuals, among others.

Liability Caps

A number of market participants and academics, and a recent report commissioned by Senator Charles Schumer and New York City Mayor Michael Bloomberg have recently advocated placing caps on auditors' potential liability as a means of reducing the risk of litigation that could lead to the loss of another large audit firm.[59] Liability caps would limit the overall amount that an audit firm would have to pay in connection with a lawsuit involving the work it performed for one of its public company clients. Some of the proposals have suggested caps that are fixed across the entire market, while others would base caps on the fees the auditor received or the client's market capitalization. Some have argued that caps would not only decrease litigation risk but would also increase the availability of insurance. Both of these developments could reduce the risk of a firm failing because of litigation. In addition, some believe liability caps could also lead to increased efficiencies if audit firms could reduce the amount of time they spent protecting themselves against lawsuits.

While some market participants thought that capping auditors' liability would be beneficial, others pointed out that such caps could have negative effects and would not protect firms against all risks that could lead to failure. Some of the former regulators and a representative of investors we spoke with were concerned that having less potential liability would limit the extent to which audit firms were held responsible for their work and could lead to lower audit quality. Others were concerned that caps would limit investors' ability to recoup losses they incurred if an auditor was found to have committed fraud. In addition, caps would not reduce the risk that firms face from enforcement actions, which could also lead to failure. Finally, a few questioned the fairness of capping liability for auditors but not for others who faced similar risk, such as public companies and investment banks.

Targeting Enforcement Actions against Responsible Individuals

As we have noted, audit firms could also fail as a result of a regulatory enforcement action, increasing market concentration. Some market participants have suggested that having regulatory or enforcement agencies target their efforts against responsible partners rather than entire organizations would reduce the risk that an audit firm might fail for this reason. DOJ has the authority to take criminal enforcement action against individuals, corporations, or partnership entities. For example, DOJ indicted Arthur Andersen as a firm for obstruction of justice in 2002, but also indicted four current or former Ernst and Young partners in 2007 for alleged tax fraud conspiracy and other charges related to marketing tax shelters. In 2005, DOJ indicted 19 individuals, including 16 former KPMG partners, on charges related to marketing fraudulent tax shelters but recently entered into a deferred prosecution agreement with the firm itself. As part of the agreement, charges would not be brought against KPMG as long as the firm followed the terms and conditions of the agreement, which included agreeing to pay $456 million in fines, restitution, and penalties.[60] Advocates of targeting the responsible individuals rather than the firm argue that DOJ should consider the negative consequences for public companies of further consolidation against the benefits of criminal indictment against a firm. DOJ guidance states that prosecutors must consider, among other factors, whether an indictment would cause "disproportionate harm" to employees who have not been proven personally culpable and the effect of prosecution on the public in determining whether to charge a firm. DOJ officials declined to comment on whether they took the potential negative consequences of firm failure into consideration when making decisions in the Ernst and Young and KPMG cases or whether they would do so in similar cases in the future.

However, others did not think that the ability of regulatory or enforcement agencies to take certain actions against audit firms should be limited. Market participants generally agreed that the facts and circumstances of each case should determine whether regulatory and enforcement agencies should take action against responsible partners or firms. One former regulator commented that removing the option of taking criminal action against a firm would give those firms safe harbor to commit fraud. Further, this proposal would not address the risk that firms face from class-action lawsuits, which is thought to be a significant portion of firms' total litigation risks

Other Proposals to Reduce Auditors' Liability for Alleged Wrongdoing

One proposal would seek to reduce the potential for further concentration due to the loss of an audit firm by changing how auditors attest to the fairness of financial statements. Officials from the six largest accounting firms and proponents of this proposal stated in a paper on serving global markets that what auditors could reasonably uncover in an audit was limited.[61] However, the attestation that auditors currently make states, "In our opinion, the financial statements present fairly, in all material respects, the financial position of the company ... and the results of its cash flows" which one commenter said fails to convey the uncertainty associated with financial statements and audits. The accounting firm paper on serving global markets states that, in the current environment, company managers, investors, and others may have expectations for audits that are too high—for example, that an auditor has detected all possible fraud in a company's financial statements. Thus, some propose changing the format and wording of the auditor's attestation to reflect the varying certainty that an auditor can give to different parts of financial statements. Some market participants we interviewed believed that including more descriptive information in the attestation would be helpful, while several others thought such a change would not make a difference in firms' liability risk and could make the attestation complex and confusing.

Another proposal, this one involving financial statement insurance, has also been suggested as a means of reducing auditors' litigation risk. Instead of having companies appoint and pay for their own external auditors, this proposal advocates creating financial statement insurance that would be provided by insurance companies. This insurance would provide coverage for investors in the public company against losses suffered as a result of problems with the company's published financial statements. Insurance companies, to lower their risk of such losses, would then appoint and pay audit firms to attest to the accuracy of the financial statements. The auditors' opinions would assist the insurance companies in setting future premiums and coverage levels.

Such financial statement insurance may be a way of lowering the risk of the loss of another large audit firm because auditors would be agents of the insurance companies. Depending on how relevant laws regulating financial statement insurance were structured, proponents note that liability would generally be shifted to insurers and away from auditors. Further, because each policy would be tailored to a particular audit engagement, one proponent has argued that more insurance than is currently available would be available under this proposal, although some risky companies may not be able to obtain it. However, most of the market participants we discussed this proposal with did not favor it, citing the significant changes it would make to the current audit function and federal securities laws and the fact that insurance companies themselves might not be interested in insuring financial statements in this way or qualified to do so.

Proposed Actions to Help Reduce the Challenges Facing Smaller Firms Would Offer Limited Benefits

Various entities have made proposals intended to help smaller firms expand their share of the audit market for public companies. These include allowing outside ownership, creating a shared experts office, standardizing licensing and registration standards, and establishing an accounting firm accreditation program.

Outside Ownership of Accounting Firms

Some market participants have suggested that allowing parties other than the firm's partners to own or invest in audit firms could increase these firms' financial resources and allow them to hire the additional staff needed to serve larger companies. According to AICPA, under all states' laws, certified public accountants (CPAs) must make up the majority ownership of all accounting firms, and other owners must be active participants in the firms.[62] These requirements were intended to preserve audit quality by ensuring auditor independence according to one market participant and an industry report.

Market participants pointed out the potential negative effects of allowing outside ownership of accounting firms, and most of the accounting firms responding to our survey agreed that being able to raise capital from such sources would have little if any effect on their ability to expand their market share.[63] Opponents of extending outside ownership argue that, without CPAs as majority owners, external shareholders might make business decisions in a firm's economic interests that compromise its independence for purposes of performing audits. One report recommending consideration of changing outside ownership rules indicated that appropriate safeguards would be needed to ensure independence and audit quality. Several of the midsize and smaller firms we interviewed said that access to capital did not pose a significant impediment to expansion, because firms currently raised sufficient capital through traditional channels such as loans backed by the partnership and, in some cases, alternative practice structures. In fact, 61 percent of midsize and smaller firm survey respondents said that increasing their access to capital would be only slightly effective or not at all effective in helping them increase the number of audit clients they served. Firms told us that the shortage of qualified accountants in the labor market rather than limited access to capital was their primary impediment to growth.

Shared Experts Office

Creating a shared entity staffed with accounting experts with specialized technical and industry expertise to supplement smaller firms' technical capabilities for performing public company audits could provide midsize and smaller firms with advice on accounting standards and audit procedures. A shared experts office could be similar in concept to the "national offices" maintained by larger firms to provide advice to their staff auditors on complex and emerging issues. According to some market participants, smaller audit firms can currently obtain assistance through various technical support services offered by FASB, AICPA, SEC, and networks or affiliations they may be a member of. But some market participants told us that services such as those the SEC provides were not heavily used, either because auditors and companies feared reprisals if they alerted regulators to potential problems they might be facing or because they did not expect a timely response.[64]

Market participants we interviewed noted that creating a shared experts office that many firms could use would have various advantages and disadvantages. Several market participants said a shared experts office that provided comprehensive support and guidance on complex accounting and auditing issues could be effective, especially if it were established within an appropriate organization. However, most did not think that establishing such an office would be feasible. Some market participants that we interviewed said that a shared office's effectiveness would be limited. For instance, one participant noted that a shared experts office would lack the "tone at the top" that a firm's national office provides. Others noted that staff at an external office could find it difficult to obtain all the needed facts from firms in order to make an accurate determination. Also, market participants said that the shortage of individuals with the required expertise could make establishing an external office challenging. Finally, some market participants said that such an office would face challenges because it could face legal liability if its staff gave out erroneous guidance that resulted in criminal or civil litigation. Furthermore, other organizations such as AICPA have considered establishing similar offices in the past but did not because they could not identify ways to overcome these challenges.[65]

Finally, midsize and smaller firms responding to our survey had mixed views on the effectiveness of this proposal as a means of expanding the number of public companies they could audit. Only 8 percent of midsize and smaller firms said that having access to specialized technical and industry expertise would be very effective in helping them expand their public company client base, and 55 percent said that it would be somewhat or moderately effective.

Uniform Licensing and Registration Standards

Easing restrictions that hindered their ability to operate in multiple states could potentially increase the ability of smaller accounting firms to serve more public company clients. Many accounting firm officials and industry groups have said that differences in auditor licensing and registration standards across states are costly and make operating in multiple jurisdictions burdensome. AICPA and the National Association of State Boards of Accountancy (NASBA) have developed the Uniform Accountancy Act, a suggested model for state legislation that was recently amended to provide a comprehensive system under which CPAs would have mobility to practice in more than one state with minimal barriers. However, each state will have to implement these changes identically to create the uniform system, and some market participants we interviewed said that states are unlikely to do so. The AICPA is working with NASBA and the state boards of accountancy to develop uniform legislation and accountancy rules in each state to eliminate some of the barriers that exist for CPAs who perform work across state lines. If the current initiative is successful, the regulatory burdens associated with licensing will be significantly improved. However, such a system is not likely to help reduce concentration because some firms we interviewed said that although complying with varying state standards was challenging, it did not prevent them from competing for new clients or entering new markets.

Accounting Firm Accreditation

Finally, providing more information about the capabilities of midsize and smaller firms could make public companies more aware of lesser-known firms and potentially increase these companies' willingness to consider additional firms as their auditor. Some market participants have suggested that establishing an accounting firm accreditation program would help establish midsize and smaller firms' reputations by providing companies and investors with additional information about their audit capabilities. An accreditation program could be similar to the programs used for colleges and universities, which use nationally recognized accrediting agencies to determine whether institutions meet established standards and thus acceptable levels of quality. Accounting firm accreditation, whether carried out by a government agency or approved private organization, could use a similar approach to certify firms as being able to audit certain types of companies.

Company officials and other market participants told us that having additional information about unfamiliar firms could be beneficial. For example, investors told us they tended to prefer firms with well-established reputations and that conducting due diligence on the unknown firms' qualifications required extra work. Several other market participants thought that providing additional information about firms through an accreditation program could be at least a moderately effective and feasible way to establish firms' reputations. One accounting firm official thought that having a credible organization endorsing firms as qualified to conduct audits for companies of certain sizes would help companies make informed decisions and increase their choices of auditors.

However, other market participants raised concerns about the costs and burden that accreditation would impose on firms. For example, according to Department of Education guidelines universities have to complete an in-depth self-evaluation that measures their performance against the established standards and undergo on-site evaluations in order to earn accreditation. Following accreditation, the accrediting body monitors and periodically reevaluates the universities' accreditation status. Some participants thought that the burden of this process could outweigh any benefits.

Appendix I

OBJECTIVES, SCOPE, AND METHODOLOGY

This work was conducted under the Comptroller General's authority. Our objectives were to study (1) the level of concentration among the market for public company audits and the impact of this concentration, (2) the potential for increased capacity among midsize and smaller accounting firms to ease market concentration, and (3) proposals that have been offered by others for easing concentration in the market for public company audits and the barriers facing midsize and smaller firms in expanding their market share for public company audits.

We conducted this performance audit in New York City and Washington, D.C., from October 2006 to January 2008 in accordance with generally accepted government auditing standards. Those standards require that we plan and perform the audit to obtain sufficient, appropriate evidence to provide a reasonable basis for our findings and conclusions based on our audit objectives. We believe that the evidence obtained provides a reasonable basis for our findings and conclusions based on our audit objectives.

To determine the level of concentration among the market for public company audits and its effect we collected data and calculated our own descriptive statistics for analysis. Using audit market data from various sources, we analyzed auditor changes and changes in audit fees, computed concentration ratios and Hirschman-Herfindahl indexes, and conducted trend analyses. We also developed and employed an econometric model to analyze the relationship between concentration and fees. Appendix V contains more details about this model. To augment these data, we interviewed academics, private consultants, trade associations, accounting firms, public companies, and Securities and Exchange Commission (SEC) and Public Company Accounting Oversight Board

(PCAOB) officials. We also reviewed relevant academic literature. Most of the research studies citied in this report have been published in academic journals. These studies were also reviewed by our economists, who determined that they did not raise serious methodological concerns and were reliable for our limited purpose. However, the inclusion of these studies is purely for research purposes and does not imply that we deem them definitive. Finally, we surveyed public companies and accounting firms about their views on these topics. Our work did not include evaluating the quality or viability of the accounting firms that perform public company audits.

To determine the potential for the growth of midsize and smaller firms to affect concentration in the market for public company audits we reviewed relevant literature and included questions on this topic in our survey of public companies and accounting firms. In addition, we obtained data on the auditors chosen by initial public offerings (IPO) from SEC filings and analyzed this data. We also analyzed data related to the size of the largest, midsize, and smaller firms. We assessed the reliability of this data and found that it was reasonably sufficient for our purposes. We also interviewed representatives of accounting firms, public companies, investment banks, institutional investors, venture capital firms, and trade associations.

To determine what proposals have been offered to address further concentration and the challenges midsize and smaller firms face we reviewed academic literature, as well as government and industry papers, and interviewed representatives of accounting firms, public companies, and other industry participants. We obtained information about the effectiveness, feasibility, and overall benefit of these proposals through our survey results and individual and group interviews with representatives from accounting firms, public companies, investment banks, institutional investors, academics, insurance companies, and former SEC officials. We also met with officials from SEC, PCAOB, and the Department of Justice (DOJ) to obtain their views on the advantages and disadvantages of these proposals. We obtained much of this information at a roundtable discussion we held on July 10, 2007, that involved 18 market participants from across all the sectors mentioned above. The overall objectives of the roundtable were to provide an opportunity for the participants from different sectors and viewpoints to engage in an in depth discussion of the significance of concentration in the market, challenges facing midsize and smaller firms, and the strengths and weaknesses of proposals previously identified, as well as to identify additional proposals. To encourage open and candid input from the various parties, we agreed not to attribute any input from either our general data collection effort or the roundtable to specific organizations or individuals.

DATA ANALYSIS

To address the structure of the audit market we computed concentration ratios and Hirschman-Herfindahl indexes (HHI) for 2000 to 2006 using Audit Analytics, an online market intelligence service maintained by Ives Group, Incorporated. Audit Analytics provides, among other things, a database of audit fees by company since 2000, along with demographic and financial information. We also used the Audit Analytics database to analyze changes in the audit fees companies have paid by various size categories. Audit Analytics also provides a comprehensive listing of all reported auditor changes that includes data on the date of change, departing auditor, engaged auditor, nature of the change (dismissal or resignation), any going concern flags or other accounting issues, and any fee disputes or fee reductions. Using this database, we identified 5,867 auditor changes from January 2003 through June 30, 2007. For our econometric model we also used data on audit opinions (going concern opinions), restatements, 404 compliance (internal control), and late filers that were also maintained by Ives Group in the Audit Analytics database. We used *Public Accounting Report* (PAR) and other sources for the remaining trend and descriptive analyses, including the analyses of the top and lower sizes of accounting firms, contained in the report.

In addition to reviewing the data collection methods and management controls over these databases that we conducted for a previous report, we assessed the reliability of the current data in other ways. We performed several checks to verify the reliability of the Audit Analytics databases. For example, we crosschecked random samples from each of the Audit Analytics databases with SEC proxy and annual filings and other publicly available information. Additionally, we compared our HHI calculations based on Audit Analytics data to HHI calculations based on the Who Audits America database, a directory of public companies with detailed information for each company, including the auditor of record, maintained by Spencer Phelps of Data Financial Press. We also spoke with other users of the Audit Analytics data. While we determined that these data were sufficiently reliable for the purpose of presenting trends in audit fees and auditor changes, as we have previously reported, the descriptive statistics on audit fees contained in the report should be viewed in light of a number of data challenges. First, the Audit Analytics audit fee database does not include fees for companies that did not disclose audit fees paid to their independent auditor in an SEC filing.[1] Second, some companies included in the database—especially small companies—did not report complete financial data. We handled missing data by dropping companies with incomplete financial data from any analysis involving the use of such data. As a result, we are not dealing with the entire population included in the Audit Analytics database but rather with a large subset. Because of these issues, the results should be viewed as estimates of audit fees and market concentration based on a large sample rather than precise estimates based on the entire population. Moreover, the sample we used to produce the estimates throughout the report does not include funds, trusts, nonoperating companies, or subsidiaries of another public company.

For a previous report we performed similar, albeit more limited, tests on PAR data, and concluded that they were appropriate for its use in this report. However, these data are self-reported by the accounting firms, which are not subject to the same reporting and financial disclosure requirements as SEC registrants. Moreover, while the data are suitable for comparing the largest firms to midsize and smaller firms, caution should be used in comparing midsize and smaller firms to each other.

To assess the market for new publicly traded companies we obtained data using SEC's Electronic Data Gathering, Analysis and Retrieval (EDGAR) system, a database that includes information on registered companies' initial public offering (IPO) in the United States. SEC's EDGAR database is the primary source for information on IPOs since all companies issuing securities that list on the major exchanges, OTC Bulletin Board (OTCBB), as well as those that meet certain criteria for listing on the Pink Sheets, must register securities with the SEC. In a previous report, we crosschecked these data with NASDAQ data on NASDAQ IPOs for consistency. For our analysis of size of the companies going public and their auditor of record, we dropped companies from our analysis that were missing the requisite revenue data in the database. We looked at a sample of these companies and concluded that companies dropped from our sample are largely companies that used either pro forma or partial year revenues in their preliminary filings, or were funds, trusts or banks. While funds and trust have been eliminated in our empirical work in this report, some publicly traded banks have also been excluded in our analysis of IPOs by size. As dropping these companies still left a large sample from which we computed the descriptive statistics contained in our report, this data limitation is minor in the context of this report.

SURVEY DATA

To augment our empirical analysis, we conducted two confidential surveys to obtain information from accounting firms and their public company clients. First, we surveyed a random sample of 595 publicly held companies. We created this population from the Audit Analytics database. Our initial population included over 6,900 U.S.-based public companies that traded on major exchanges (NYSE, NASDAQ, AMEX, OTCBB), excluding foreign filers, funds and trusts, and benefit plans. Our sample was allocated across six strata: (1) large companies (Fortune 1000) that had changed auditors since 2003, (2) medium-size companies (greater than $75 million in market capitalization, but not Fortune 1000) that had changed auditors since 2003, (3) small companies (less than $75 million in market capitalization) that had changed auditors since 2003, (4) large companies that had not changed auditors since 2003, (5) medium-size companies that had not changed auditors since 2003, and (6) small companies that had not changed auditors since 2003. The survey included questions related to companies' audit services and the selection and engagement of the company's auditor. To develop the questionnaire, we consulted with individuals knowledgeable about the accounting profession, including representatives of Financial Executives International and public companies. We also pretested our questionnaire with three public companies of different sizes and industries. We directed our survey to the audit committee chair—or other member of the audit committee—where available. We obtained names and addresses for audit committee members from Audit Analytics. If no audit committee information was available, we conducted additional research and identified a member of the company's management, typically the chief financial officer, as the recipient of the questionnaire.

We mailed paper questionnaires on May 22, 2007. Those companies not completing the questionnaire were sent a replacement questionnaire and another reminder letter in June and July. On June 12 and 13, we also made phone calls to the corporate headquarters of 210 companies whose audit committee chair or other selected informant had not responded in an attempt to reach that person to encourage response. After excluding 29 sampled companies that we found to be ineligible for the population, we received 406 usable responses as of August 15, 2007 from the final sample of 566 companies, for an overall response rate of 73 percent (table 3). Again, the number of responses to individual questions may fluctuate, depending on how many respondents answered each question.

Table 3. Disposition of Public Company Sample

	Companies that changed auditor since 2003			Companies that have not changed auditor since 2003			
	Fortune 1000	Non-Fortune 1000, with market capitalization of $75 million or greater	Non-Fortune 1000, with market capitalization of less than $75 million	Fortune 1000	Non-Fortune 1000, with market capitalization of $75 million or greater	Non-Fortune 1000, with market capitalization of less than $75 million	All companies
Initial population	80	917	1,682	792	2,295	1,140	6,906
Initial sample	58	70	124	81	178	84	595
Ineligibles detected in the sample	1	5	14	1	4	4	29
Final eligible Population	78	832	1,405	778	2,228	1,061	6,383
Final eligible sample	57	65	110	80	174	80	566
Usable responses	42	49	71	56	134	54	406
Response rate (number of responses divided by final eligible sample)	74%	77%	69%	70%	78%	69%	73%

Source: GAO.

The public company survey results came from a random sample drawn from our population of U.S. publicly traded companies and, thus, could be weighted to statistically represent that larger group. We weighted our sample to adjust for nonresponse by company size. In our analysis, we did detect a small amount of nonresponse bias among small public companies traded over the counter. We analyzed the result of this nonresponse on selected estimates. We concluded that the nonresponse did not affect our findings or conclusions. Unless otherwise noted, the margin of error for public company survey results used in the report was less than 12 percentage points.

Second, we surveyed representatives of a take-all sample of the entire population—437 midsize and smaller U.S. accounting firms that audited at least one public company in 2006 (as identified by information in the Audit Analytics database) and were also registered with PCAOB. Each of the midsize firms operates nationally and to some extent internationally, audits more than 100 public companies, and has around $1 billion in revenue or less. The smaller firms audit regional and local public companies and have fewer than 100 public company clients. We used the survey to obtain firms' views on their plans regarding engagements with public companies, participation in associations, competition, audit costs and quality, and related issues. We obtained name and address information for the executives to be contacted from registration applications filed with PCAOB.[2] To develop our questionnaire, we consulted a number of experts knowledgeable about the accounting profession, including representatives of PCAOB. We also pretested our questionnaire with one of the four largest firms, a midsize firm, and two smaller firms.

We began our Web-based survey on May 16, 2007, and included all usable responses as of August 15, 2007 to produce this report. After we removed three firms found to be ineligible for the survey (merged out of existence, or without at least one publicly held U.S. client), the final eligible population we surveyed was 434 firms. See table 4 for the final disposition of our sample, including the subset of firms with five or more publicly held clients that we chose to report statistics for in this product.

Table 4. Disposition of Accounting Firms Selected for Survey

	Five or more clients	One to four clients	Total
Initial sample	181	256	437
Ineligibles outside the survey population	0	3	3
Final eligible sample	181	253	434
Refusals	2	8	10
Other nonresponse	61	112	173
Usable responses	118	133	251
Response rate (number of responses divided by final eligible sample)	65%	53%	58%

Source: GAO.

Those firms not completing the questionnaire were sent up to four emails starting on June 1, 2007, and a sample of firms not responding were called to attempt to gain their participation on June 13 and 14. A paper version of the questionnaire was provided upon request, and firms could respond using this questionnaire by fax or mail.

We received 251 usable responses from these 434 firms, for an overall response rate of 58 percent. However, the number of responses to individual questions may be fewer than 251, depending on how many responding firms were eligible or chose to answer a particular question. In addition, we determined during our pretests that many of the survey questions were irrelevant for the largest firms, so we administered selected survey questions orally to representatives of each of the largest firms and conducted indepth individual interviews with representatives of each of these firms. That information is reported separately from the firm survey results.

While the accounting firm survey results came from a census of the population, we limited our analysis in this report to the 118 responding firms with 5 or more publicly held clients because the response rate of firms with only 1-4 clients was significantly lower (53 percent) than for the larger firms (65 percent). Our analysis suggested that those small firms responding were different from those that did not, in terms of geography and number of clients. We were concerned that some small firms did not respond because the prospect of more auditing work for publicly held clients did not appeal to them and, thus, they found the survey request irrelevant. The small firms that responded could have answered the survey questions differently than the nonresponding small firms would have. As a result, reporting percentages based on responding small firms with one to four clients could introduce bias into results if those results were generalized to all accounting firms that audited at least one publicly traded company.

In addition to potential nonresponse bias, there are other practical difficulties in conducting any survey that may contribute to errors in survey results. For example, differences in how a question is interpreted or the sources of information available to respondents can introduce unwanted variability into the survey results. We included steps in both the data collection and data analysis stages to minimize such errors. In addition to the questionnaire testing and development measures mentioned above, we followed up with the firms and clients with letters, e-mails, and telephone calls to encourage them to respond and offer assistance. Before the surveys began, we mailed notification letters to both survey samples, encouraging them to respond and asking them to correct improper contact information. We also checked and edited the survey data and programs used to produce our survey results. In addition to the survey statistics cited in this report, all survey questions and the frequencies of responses to each question are presented in a supplemental product that can be found on our Web site at http://www.gao.gov/cgi-bin/getrpt?GAO-08-164SP.

Appendix II

Other Issues Related to Concentration in the Audit Market

Although having eased slightly recently, the overall market for public company audits continues to be highly concentrated among the largest accounting firms. In assessing the degree of concentration in a market, the standard practice uses the proportion of each competing firm's share of the overall revenue collected. By analyzing data from Audit Analytics, which collects audit information from the filings public companies submit to the Securities and Exchange Commission (SEC), we found that the overall extent to which the largest firms dominate the amount of total audit fees collected continues to be very high. As shown in table 5, 94 percent of the total amount of audit fees paid by public companies went to the largest firms in 2006.[1] This is slightly lower than the 96 percent of audit fees the largest firms earned in 2002. As a result, the general market can still be characterized as a tight oligopoly, which is a market dominated by a small number of sellers with the risk that these firms could greatly influence price and other market factors.[2]

Table 5. Market Shares of Audit Fees by Accounting Firm Size

	2002	2004	2006
Largest	96.2%	96.4%	94.4%
Midsize	1.5%	1.7%	2.7%
Smaller	2.3%	1.9%	2.9%

Source: GAO analysis of Audit Analytics data.

Note: Data do not include trusts, mutual funds, blank check or nonoperating entities. Companies paying audit fees to two different auditors in one year are also excluded.

The largest firms are significantly larger than their nearest competitors. According to data from the Public Accounting Report, which collects self-reported financial information from accounting firms, the combined audit revenue of the four midsize firms is slightly less than one-half the audit revenue of the smallest of the largest firms.[3] Similarly, as shown in figure 11, the market share as measured by audit fees of each of the largest firms individually is much larger than the market share of the other groups combined.

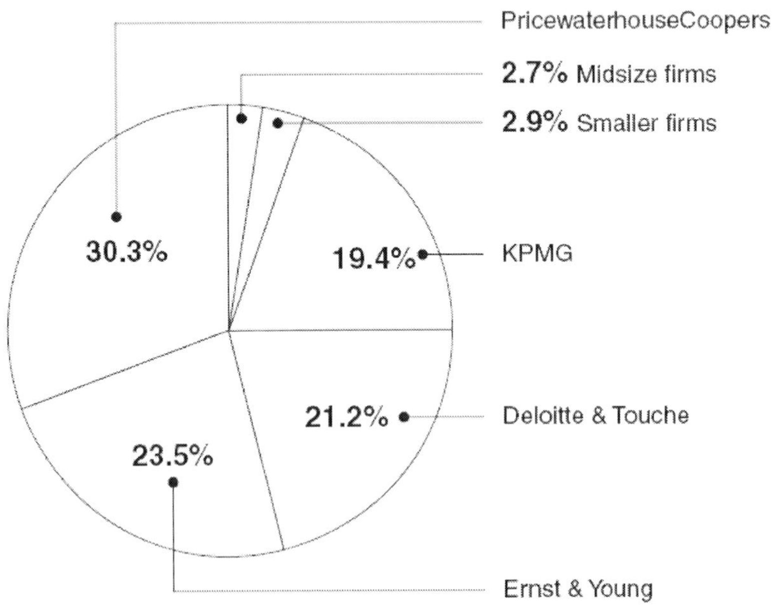

Source: GAO analysis of Audit Analytics data.

Note: Figure does not include trusts, funds, blank check or nonoperating entities. Companies paying audit fees to two different auditors in one year are also excluded.

Figure 11: 2006 Market Shares of Each of the Largest Firms Compared to Other Firms, as Measured by Audit Fees.

Overall Audit Market and Many Specific Industries Are Highly Concentrated

Another key statistical measure that is used to assess the degree to which a market is dominated by relatively few firms also shows that the public company audit market is highly concentrated. The Hirschman-Herfindahl Index (HHI) is one of the concentration measures used by government agencies, such as DOJ and the Federal Trade Commission, to aid in the assessment of market structure and potential market power. An HHI for a market is calculated using the various market shares of the firms competing to offer goods or services within it.[4] According to merger guidelines issued by DOJ, an HHI below 1,000 indicates a market that is predisposed to perform competitively and one that is unlikely to have adverse competitive effects. An HHI between 1,000 and 1,800 indicates a moderately concentrated market, while an HHI above 1,800 indicates a highly concentrated market.

As shown in figure 12, the HHI in 2006 for the overall market for public company audits—as determined based on the audit fees collected by accounting firms auditing public companies—was 2,300, a level considered to be significantly concentrated. This represents a slight decline since 2002, when the audit market's HHI was around 2,390 after it peaked following the dissolution of Arthur Andersen.[5]

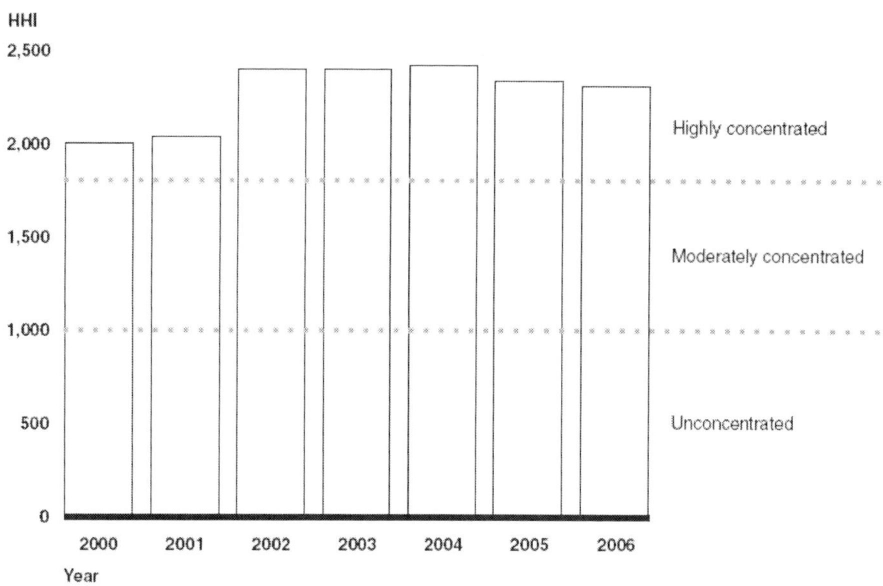

Source: GAO analysis of Audit Analytics data.
Note: HHI figures based on total audit fees.

Figure 12. Hirschman-Herfindahl Indexes, 2000-2006.

We also found that analyzing the audit market by region and industry reveals that many industries were similarly highly concentrated and that concentration also exists across six major geographic regions of the country.[6] We segmented the market into distinct economic sector (industry) audits and distinct regional audits. As figure 13 illustrates, all industries are above the threshold for significant market power and have generally shown some improvement since 2002, but some sectors are significantly more concentrated than others. A number of these industry-specific markets would not only be considered tight oligopolies but would also be considered dominant firm markets (one firm holding over 60 percent of the market with no significant competitors). For example, Ernst and Young accounts for 77 percent of all audit fees collected in the agricultural sector while, the second largest firm only holds 12 percent of the market.

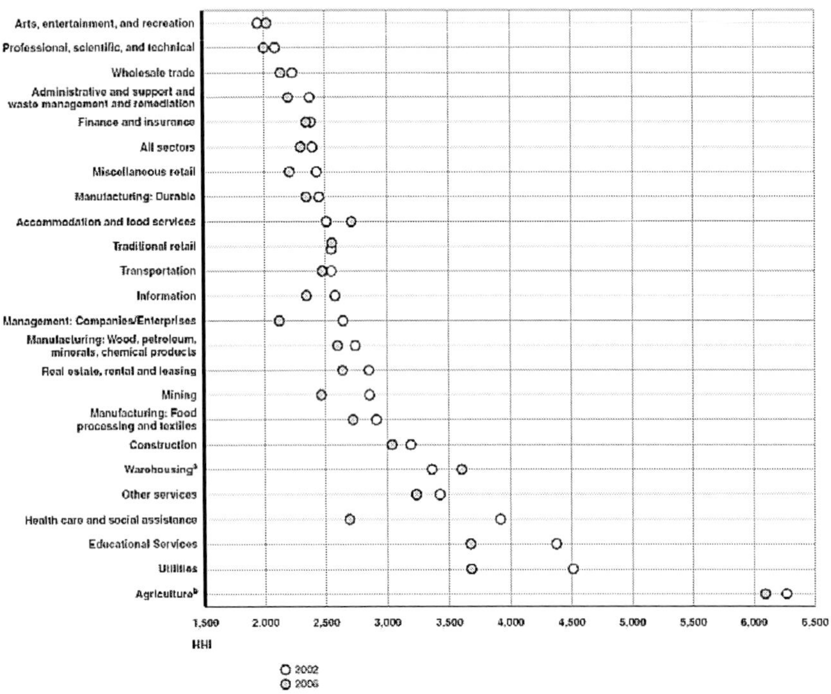

Source: GAO analysis of Audit Analytics data.

Notes: Industries defined by two digit North American Industry Classification System codes.

[a] The warehousing sector contains fewer than 15 companies.

[b] The agriculture sector has fewer than 30 companies.

Figure 13. Hirschman-Herfindahl Indexes, Markets Segmented by Industry.

Similarly, we found regional markets in the United States such the Mid-Atlantic and the Midwest to be somewhat more concentrated than the Western regions, although all were highly concentrated.[7]

Loss of One of the Largest Firms Would Result in Even Higher Concentration

In the event of further mergers, acquisitions, or closures of large firms, the market would become even more concentrated. To determine the effect of further concentration, we simulated the effect of the failure or exit of one of the largest firms and the effect of a merger between two of the largest firms.[8] When simulating the effect of the failure or exit of the smallest of the largest firms, we distributed the clients of the failed firm among the remaining firms in the same proportion as the clients of Arthur Andersen were distributed after that firm dissolved. Under this scenario, the resulting HHI of the overall audit market would rise from 2,300 to roughly 3,000 which is considerably further above what DOJ considers to be a concentrated market (figure 14). Further, figure 14 shows that if we segment the audit market by size, that the increase in HHI would be greatest among large companies. Higher concentration could increase the risk that the remaining large accounting firms could exercise market power to raise prices and coordinate their actions among themselves to the detriment of their clients.

The figure also shows that a merger between two of the largest firms could significantly increase concentration for the overall audit market. To identify the result of such a merger, we simulated the effect of a merger between the two smallest of the largest firms and found that HHI for the market as a whole would increase from 2,300 to 3,124, which is again well above DOJ's threshold for a concentrated market and higher than in the case of a firm failure. As with the case of a firm failure, segmenting the audit market by size illustrates the biggest increase in HHI would occur in the market for large public company audits, which according to our simulation would rise from 2,558 to 3,476 (figure 14).

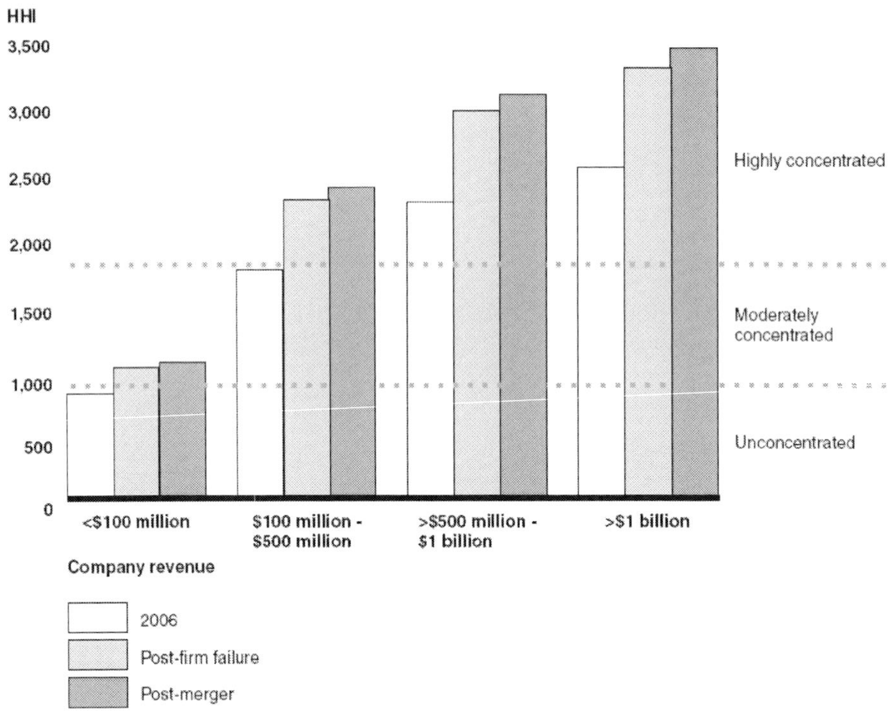

Source: GAO analysis of Audit Analytics data.

Figure 14. HHI with Simulated Firm Failure or Merger.

Appendix III

Analysis of Auditor Changes

In the last few years, companies that changed their auditor switched to a midsize or smaller accounting firm more frequently than to one of the largest firms. We analyzed data from the Audit Analytics database of over 8,000 auditor changes among companies registered with the Securities and Exchange Commission (SEC) and listed on major exchanges (NYSE, NASDAQ and AMEX), as well as those traded through other exchanges such as OTCBB. Through this analysis, we identified 5,867 total changes in auditors between January 2003 and June 2007.[1] As shown in table 6, the largest firms lost a net total of 1,149 clients, while the midsize and smaller firms picked up a net total of 282 and 867 clients, respectively.

Table 6 also shows that while midsize and smaller firms gained a larger number of clients, the largest firms still retained the clients that, on average, have higher revenues and pay larger audit fees than the companies that switched to a midsize or smaller firm. Therefore, despite the largest firms experiencing a net loss of over one thousand clients, most of these were smaller companies with lower revenues and audit fees. Companies that changed from one of the largest firms to another had average revenues of over $1 billion, while companies that changed from one of the largest firms to a smaller firm had average revenues of just over $60 million.

Table 6. Public Companies Changing Accounting Firms, January 2003 to June 2007

	Accounting firm after change			Total
Accounting firm	Largest	Midsize	Smaller	departures
Largest				
Number of companies leaving largest firms	561	560	742	1,863
Average revenue of largest firms' clients	$1,687,884,613	$170,386,590	$60,857,991	
Average audit fee paid by largest firms' clients	$2,013,663	$549,825	$227,901	
Midsize				
Number of companies leaving midsize firms	52	45	342	439
Average revenue of midsize firms' clients	$581,263,262	$84,047,669	$34,511,234	
Average audit fee paid by midsize firms' clients	$820,200	$300,287	$151,511	
Smaller				
Number of companies leaving smaller firms	101	116	3,348	3,565
Average revenue of smaller firms' clients	$106,434,760	$40,328,634	$6,045,755	
Average audit fee paid by clients	$431,124	$213,265	$52,885	
Total gains[a]	153	676	1,084	
Total losses[b]	(1,302)	(394)	(217)	
Net gain (loss)	(1,149)	282	867	

Source: GAO analysis of Audit Analytics data.

Notes: Average revenue and average audit fee figures are based only on those companies with available relevant financial data.

[a] Total gains represent the sum of companies that went to that particular category of accounting firm (largest, midsize, or smaller) from another category. For example, the largest accounting firms gained 153 companies from 2003 to 2007 (52 from midsize firms and 101 from smaller firms).

[b] Total losses represent the sum of companies that left that particular category of accounting firm (largest, midsize, or smaller) for another category. For example, large accounting firms lost 1,302 companies from 2003 to 2007 (560 went to midsize firms and 742 went to smaller firms).

Table 7. Percentage and Number of Changes Public Companies Made in Auditors, by Region

Engaged Auditor	Percentage of companies changing auditors gained or lost						
	Mid-Atlantic	New England	Southeast	Midwest	Southwest	West	Total
Largest	14.11%	20.91%	10.44%	19.63%	10.36%	9.27%	12.16%
	(-261)	(-84)	(-179)	(-152)	(-110)	(-360)	(-1,149)
Midsize	13.49%	13.94%	11.38%	27.23%	11.18%	8.25%	12.29%
	(75)	(11)	(49)	(88)	(28)	(31)	(282)
Smaller	72.41%	65.16%	78.18%	53.15%	78.44%	82.48%	75.54%
	(186)	(73)	(130)	(64)	(82)	(329)	(867)

Source: GAO analysis of Audit Analytics data.

Note: Changes in auditors where region was unknown were excluded.

Within these changes, we also found that midsize firms gained clients in particular regions and industries. Overall, as shown in table 7, the largest firms lost clients in every region of the United States (Mid-Atlantic, New England, Southeast, Midwest, Southwest, and West). In contrast, the midsize firms experienced net gains in clients in all of these regions, especially in the Midwest where they acquired 27 percent of the companies that changed auditors. Smaller firms also added clients in all regions, most notably in the West, where 329 additional companies selected them to serve as the auditor of record. This represents 82 percent of the changes made in that region. Incidentally, the Western region is also the area in which the largest firms suffered their worst losses and the midsize firms generally experienced their weakest gains.

Our analysis of companies that ultimately selected one of the largest firms or a midsize firm shows that midsize firms have made inroads into certain industry sectors. In sectors in which there were at least 30 changes, Grant Thornton captured more than 20 percent of the companies that switched in mining; certain manufacturing; wholesale trade; information; professional, scientific, and technical services; and accommodation and food services. BDO Seidman also secured over 20 percent of the changes in six sectors with at least 30 changes: certain manufacturing; wholesale trade; information; professional, scientific, and technical services; management of companies and enterprises; and administrative, support, and waste management and remediation services. Finally, Crowe Chizek was the only firm in the top eight to engage more than 20 percent of the finance and insurance companies that switched to one of the largest firms or a midsize firm.

Companies reported a number of different reasons for changing auditors. According to our survey results, large companies that recently changed auditors frequently reported that they did so to obtain better customer service (69 percent). Many large companies also reported changing auditors to obtain a better working relationship with their auditor (67 percent). Others said they changed auditors to obtain lower fees (26 percent).

In interviews, representatives of public companies, accounting firms, and other market participants attributed many of the midsize and small company auditor changes to the aftermath of the Sarbanes-Oxley Act, which, among other things, enhanced auditor independence and required increased reviews of public companies' internal controls (which initially affected larger public companies) and prompted the largest firms to focus on providing those services to their large clients. This increased workload increased the largest firms' costs and fees and necessitated that some smaller public companies expand their options and look to midsize or smaller firms. Officials from two of the largest firms told us that they did make changes to their client portfolios in the period after Sarbanes-Oxley was passed, including resigning as auditor of record from some clients for risk or capacity constraint reasons. On our survey of the over 400 U.S. accounting firms that audit public companies, midsize and smaller accounting firms responding also reported resigning as auditor of record for risk mitigation reasons, specific issues with the client, or fees being insufficient to cover audit costs.[2] Midsize and small companies that recently changed auditors indicated on our survey that they did so to obtain better customer service, a better working relationship with their auditor, lower fees or because their auditor resigned. In addition, some companies commented that they changed because their auditor was too busy and expensive for them or because their auditor wanted to focus on larger clients. A few reported, however, that they changed auditors because the auditor went out of business or merged with another firm.[3]

Appendix IV

TRENDS IN AUDIT COSTS AND QUALITY

Various factors likely affected changes in audit fees and audit quality since the demise of Enron and Arthur Andersen. According to our data analysis, survey, and interviews, audit costs and quality seem to have increased in recent years. Additional work associated with new and increasingly complex accounting and auditing standards, cost increases associated with auditor changes and with acquiring and retaining audit staff, new costs associated with regulatory oversight of public company audits and other requirements of the Sarbanes-Oxley Act (the Act), and some firms' recovering more of their costs have likely contributed to increases in audit fees. Similarly, while many of these factors have been cited as reasons for why it has been increasingly hard for accounting firms to maintain audit quality, market participants generally agreed that these changes have contributed to improved audit quality.

FACTORS INFLUENCING AUDIT COSTS

To varying degrees, different factors likely contributed to increased audit fees since 2001 including firms' performing additional audit work, higher costs commonly associated with auditor changes and with acquiring and retaining audit staff, increases associated with the new public company audit oversight structure and auditors expanded interaction with audit committees, and firms' recovering more of their costs through audit fees. Many market participants have noted that the number and complexity of requirements associated with accounting and auditing standards have contributed to firms performing new and additional procedures to help comply with the new requirements and reduce audit and litigation risk. Since 2000, public companies and their auditor have, where applicable, had to deal with new and expanded accounting standards dealing with hedge activities, derivatives, other financial instruments, impaired assets, and intangible assets including goodwill. In addition, firms have had to deal with new and expanded audit standards related to fraud, audit documentation, and fair value measurements and disclosures.

In response to the demise of Arthur Andersen in 2002, more than 1,000 of its public company audit clients had to find new audit firms. In addition, as firms and public companies adjust to market-related changes following the 2002 Sarbanes-Oxley Act, auditor change has continued. Our analysis of auditor changes found that between 2003 and 2007 almost 6,000 auditor changes occurred. Echoing our 2003 study of audit firm rotation, some market participants we spoke to said that changing auditors would increase public company audit-related costs. As part of our 2003 study of audit firm rotation, we surveyed large (Fortune 1000) public companies and firms that audited more than 10 public companies and more than 67 percent of companies and firms responded that a change in auditor would likely increase firms' initial year audit costs and public company audit support costs—taken together—by more than 30 percent. In addition, accounting firms we have spoken to and surveyed cited increased costs of attracting and retaining talented audit staff and specialists. Many of those commenting on this factor linked the higher costs of attracting and retaining talented staff to the increased capacity-related demands facing the firms associated with implementing the Act.

Also, the Act established a new major audit requirement that has significantly expanded the scope of financial audits for public companies by requiring, among other things, that their auditor assess and report on the effectiveness of their internal control over financial reporting (Section 404b). Representatives from all sizes of accounting firms we spoke to said that the new audit requirement related to internal controls, which generally became effective for the 2004 audits of the largest public companies, has resulted in a substantial increase in their workload and related costs associated with additional audit staff and expertise, and audit methodologies. Until 2008, auditors for only the largest public companies, those considered to be accelerated filers, have had to comply with the new internal control audit-related requirements. Firms that audit smaller public companies, those considered nonaccelerated filers, are scheduled to comply with the new audit requirement with annual filings after December 15, 2008. When effective for smaller public companies, the requirement is expected to further increase their audit fees.

The accounting firms that we have spoken to noted that, in addition to requiring new internal control work; other requirements of the Act have contributed to increased audit costs and the fees charged to public companies. The Act established a new regulatory oversight structure for firms that audit public companies with the creation of the Public Company Accounting Oversight Board (PCAOB). To date, PCAOB has established firm registration and inspection programs and has adopted auditing standards that Securities and Exchange Commission (SEC) has approved that registered firms must follow. Several firms we have spoken to since the PCAOB was established noted that they have incurred additional costs to support PCAOB-related activities, as well as respond to the audit documentation standard and a shorter audit partner rotation period mandated by the Act. In addition, since a key provision of the Act made public company audit committees responsible for hiring the firm and overseeing the audit, some firms we spoke to said they have seen a substantial increase in their staffs' interaction with the audit committees members, which has added to audit costs.

A number of firms we spoke to also noted that the Act's stricter independence requirements may have contributed to higher audit fees by causing some firms to change the way they price their audit service. The stricter independence requirements were intended to significantly limit the types of nonaudit services firms can sell to their audit clients without impairing the firm's independence. Department of Justice (DOJ) officials and others we spoke to stated that the significant limits on firms' opportunities to sell audit clients nonaudit services make them less likely to under price audits as a loss leader. To the extent that firms in the past have underpriced their audits expecting to sell nonaudit services which are now prohibited, it is reasonable to believe that these firms have increased their audit fees to cover their audit cost.

The results of our survey of midsize and smaller firms and our discussions with the largest firms generally confirmed the factors that have increased the audit cost fees. All four of the largest firms reported in interviews that the increasing complexity of accounting and auditing standards and the additional requirements of new standards were factors having a significant effect on the cost of audits. The largest firms and the other firms differed only slightly on other factors that have significantly affected audit cost. The largest firms noted costs to attract and retain talented staff and costs related to litigation as the two other top factors contributing to increased audit costs. In addition to the requirements of new standards and the price of talent, the other firms cited the time and effort to prepare for the PCAOB inspection and the complexity of accounting principles and auditing standards as their top factors.

The results of our survey of the audit committee chairs of over 500 public companies also show that increases in audit hours and rates charged by firms and other factors have led to increased audit fees. Public companies that reported increasing audit fees reported that changes in the number of hours by the audit engagement team (85 percent) and senior partners (73 percent), as well as changes in hourly rates of the audit team and senior partners (76 percent), led to increased audit fees.[1] In addition, of those public companies reporting that their audit costs had increased since 2003, 84 percent reported that the additional requirement for an audit of internal control over financial reporting was a factor in the increase of their audit.

FACTORS INFLUENCING AUDIT QUALITY

While management has the primary responsibility for the quality and reliability of a public company's financial statements, the auditor is responsible for providing reasonable assurance, through an independent audit, about the reliability of the company's financial statements. Investors need to know that the financial statements on which they make investment decisions are reliable and the independent audit plays a vital role in assuring their reliability. In a prior report, we defined a quality audit as one conducted, in accordance with applicable auditing standards to provide reasonable assurance about whether the audited financial statements are presented in accordance with applicable accounting principles and are free of material misstatements.[2] Audit quality is often thought to include the experience and technical capability of the auditing firm partners and staff, the capability to efficiently respond to a client's needs, and the ability and willingness to appropriately identify and surface material reporting issues in financial reports. When high quality public company audits are performed, management and investors are more likely to rely on the financial statements and the financial information they contain.

Audit Oversight

For decades, the public accounting profession was, in practice, self-regulated, taking responsibility for establishing auditing standards and administering a program designed to oversee the activities of independent public accounting firms that audit companies whose securities are registered with the SEC. While given statutory authority for establishing rules governing financial reports for publicly traded companies in the 1930s, SEC permitted the accounting profession (American Institute of Certified Public Accountants (AICPA)) to set auditing standards, subject to SEC's oversight of the standard-setting process. Concerns raised with the audits of public companies in the 1970s focused attention on the need to improve the quality control mechanisms used by firms to ensure that professional standards were being met. In response, AICPA revised its approach to setting audit standards in 1979 by establishing the Auditing Standards Board, which was designed to have a more efficient standard-setting process through a body composed of representatives from firms of all sizes and nonpublic accounting organizations. In 1977, AICPA instituted two voluntary peer review programs—one for firms performing audits of public companies and one for those performing audits of private companies—designed to review the systems of audit quality controls for participating firms' audits of companies. Also, in 1977, AICPA created the Public Oversight Board to represent the public interest by overseeing the audit standards-setting process and the voluntary peer review program.

The purpose of the peer review program AICPA established was to provide the public with assurance that a firm performing auditing services for companies registered with SEC had an effective quality control system that provided reasonable assurance that its audits were in compliance with generally accepted auditing standards. According to the AICPA, a number of large accounting firms had been using peer reviews to enhance audit quality as far back as the early 1960s. In 1988, AICPA made peer review mandatory for all member firms performing auditing and accounting services.

To enhance auditor independence, improve audit quality, and restore investor confidence in response to the major accountability breakdowns at Enron and WorldCom, the Congress, through the enactment of the Sarbanes-Oxley Act, replaced the profession's longstanding self-regulatory structure for public company audits with an independent regulatory structure administered by PCAOB. Among its other responsibilities, the Act made PCAOB responsible for establishing auditing and other professional standards applicable to the audits of public companies by registered firms and inspecting those firms which perform public company audits. Since its establishment in 2002, PCAOB has designated certain existing auditing and quality control standards issued by the Auditing Standards Board through April 2003 as its interim standards, while focusing its attention on issuing new and modifying certain interim auditing standards. As of September 2007, PCAOB has not issued either new or modified quality control standards.

In addition to its work on standards, PCAOB is responsible, through its inspection program, for evaluating the auditor's application of existing audit and related requirements standards to promote high quality audits.[3] The PCAOB inspection program replaced the AICPA's peer review program that evaluated firms' public company auditing practices.[4]

Views on Audit Quality

Many factors can affect audit quality including auditing, accounting, and quality control standards; accounting firm inspections; and audit staff quality; and the availability of qualified audit staff. In asking accounting firms about audit quality, we considered audit quality to include the experience and technical capability of the audit firm partners and staff as well as the capability to efficiently respond to a client's needs and identify and communicate material reporting issues in financial reports. All of the largest firms and over 80 percent of the midsize and 3 accounting firms responding to our survey said that, since 2003, it has been harder to maintain audit quality.[5] This widely held view likely reflects the significant changes in the auditing environment since 2003 and the capacity demands facing the profession as audits have become more complex, requirements have expanded, and the PCAOB's inspection program has been implemented. Together these changes have increased emphasis on audit quality. Midsize and smaller accounting firms participating in our survey indicated that several factors have made it harder to maintain audit quality, with the most significant being the complexity of the accounting principles and auditing standards (92 percent), staff experience and technical capability with complex accounting principles and auditing standards (90 percent), and availability of qualified staff (84 percent). The largest firms' views on audit quality were also in line with those of the survey respondents. Representatives of all of the largest firms indicated that the complexity of the accounting principles and auditing standards and staff experience and technical capability with complex accounting principles and auditing standards have made maintaining audit quality harder. In addition, three of the four firms indicated the availability of qualified staff has made maintaining audit quality harder. During interviews, some representatives of the largest firms noted that they have significantly increased the number of staff in their national offices who provide technical consultations to the audit teams due to the complexity of the accounting principles and auditing standards. Also, during interviews, representatives of accounting firms mentioned that they have faced stiffer competition in hiring due to companies expanding their accounting and internal audit departments, SEC and PCAOB increasing their staff, and consulting firms wanting experienced accountants to help their clients implement section 404.

During our interviews, all of the largest firms and in replying to the survey, all of the midsize firms who responded, indicated that the increased role of the audit committee made maintaining audit quality easier. Only 23 percent of the smaller survey respondents shared this view.[6] Also, half of the largest and midsize firms responded that complying with PCAOB inspections made maintaining audit quality easier as compared with only 8 percent of the smaller firm survey respondents.

Despite the fact that accounting firms reported it was harder to maintain audit quality, market participants we spoke to who commented on audit quality generally noted that they thought audit quality had improved. Similarly, public companies think several aspects of audit quality have increased in recent years. In our survey to public companies, we asked about specific aspects of audit quality and how those aspects have changed since 2003.[7] While companies reported that several aspects of quality have remained the same, the aspects the public company survey respondents indicated increased most significantly were the amount of time spent by audit engagement team (77 percent), the addition of audit of internal control over financial reporting as required in the Sarbanes-Oxley Act (73 percent), and amount of time spent by senior partners and experts (72 percent). Company officials and others we interviewed also generally said that overall audit quality had increased in recent years. One controller we interviewed said that overall audit quality had become lax before the Sarbanes-Oxley Act was passed. However, he thinks that quality has changed significantly in recent years and auditors are much more rigorous. While public companies we surveyed were generally satisfied with their auditor of record considering the scope of the audit, the fees paid for audit services and the quality they received, several respondents commented that the requirements in Sarbanes-Oxley have led to significant increases in audit work and fees. Some survey respondents also questioned whether these higher costs exceeded the benefits of the additional requirements.

Appendix V

ECONOMETRIC ANALYSIS OF THE EFFECT OF INDUSTRY CONCENTRATION ON AUDIT FEES

The current structure of the market for audit services has raised concerns about the potential for anticompetitive pricing, especially for the largest public company clients. While the classic oligopoly theory suggests that prices of goods and services are positively associated with market concentration, the modern theory of industrial organization makes no clear statement regarding the impact of concentration on competition. Therefore, to investigate the relationship between concentration and audit fees, we compiled a panel data set using Audit Analytics data. The data initially contained observations on over 12,000 companies over a seven-year period from 2000 to 2006 excluding funds, trusts, and nonoperating entities. To analyze the relationship as validly as the data constraints allowed, we employed various panel data modeling techniques. While the results suggest that the increase in audit fees appears largely unrelated to supplier concentration, in part because of all the contemporaneous changes occurring in the market and other modeling and data limitations, these findings should not necessarily be viewed as definitive or as proof that that market for audit services is competitive. This appendix provides additional information on the construction of our database, econometric model, additional descriptive statistics and the limitations of the analysis.

THE PANEL DATA SAMPLE WAS CREATED BY COMPILING SEVERAL AUDIT ANALYTICS DATABASES

To construct the database used to estimate the econometric model we compiled audit fee and financial data and additional information on the thousands of public companies audited by the largest, midsize, and other public accounting firms. Audit Analytics, an online intelligence service maintained by Ives Group, Incorporated provides, among other things, a database of fees paid by public companies to their auditors back to 2000 with demographic and financial information. In addition, we added information on these companies using the Late Filer, Internal Control, Restatement, Auditor Change and Audit Opinion databases also maintained by Audit Analytics. In this manner, we were able to include information on the risk and auditing characteristics of the companies as additional control variables in the resultant econometric model. Moreover, a panel data set, that is data pooled across all companies over the 2000 to 2006 period, allowed us to account for variances in audit fees across companies and over time as well as use techniques that enhance the validity of the parameter estimates. We deleted from our sample various entities including funds, plans and trusts, subsidiaries with parent data already included in the database, blank check and nonoperating entities and duplicate entries. Table 8 reports the descriptive statistics on the resultant panel data set. Because some companies either did not exist until the later years, merged with other companies, went private, entered into bankruptcy, or otherwise failed to report at some point over the period, not all the companies have the requisite data for each year. Moreover, companies were not required to report audit fees until 2001.[1] As a result, the panel is unbalanced. The public companies clients remaining in our sample were used initially to investigate two related questions:

- When other important factors influencing audit fees are accounted for, do companies operating in more concentrated sectors of the economy pay higher fees?
- When other important factors influencing audit fees are accounted for, do companies audited by accounting firms with higher market shares in a certain sector pay higher fees?

Table 8. Descriptive Statistics of the Panel Data Set, 2000-2006

Dollars in millions	2000 N=4,440	2001 N=6,498	2002 N=8,762	2003 N=9,817	2004 N=9,863	2005 N=9,270	2006 N=8,559
Audit fees[a]							
Average	$0.651	$0.707	$0.931	$1.016	$1.431	$1.559	$1.711
Median	0.186	0.187	0.186	0.187	0.243	0.304	0.349
Standard deviation	2.134	2.341	3.673	3.671	5.158	5.022	5.395
Revenue of firms audited[a]							
Average	$2,044	$1,918	$1,888	$1,984	$2,191	$2,292	$2,551
Median	130	122	84	70	68	71	80
Standard deviation	10,295	9,209	9,024	9,946	11,444	12,044	13,154
Assets of firms audited[a]							
Average	$5,582	$5,070	$5,983	$6,476	$7,244	$7,476	$8,404
Median	312	256	188	156	160	166	190
Standard deviation	37,597	38,148	46,492	52,293	62,141	65,008	75,389
Median fees (percentage of revenue)	0.14%	0.15%	0.22%	0.27%	0.37%	0.39%	0.36%
Average fees (percentage of revenue)	0.04%	0.04%	0.06%	0.06%	0.08%	0.08%	0.08%
Median fees (percentage of assets)	0.07%	0.09%	0.14%	0.19%	0.27%	0.31%	0.29%

Source: GAO analysis of Audit Analytics data.

Notes: N is the number of observations in each year that have audit fees reported.

[a] Dollars are converted to real terms using the chain weighted GDP price index. Total audit fees include audit and audit-related fees.

Our panel data approach investigates industry (economic sector) concentration (HHI) from 2000 to 2006 since there is variation in the degree of concentration across industries and within industries over time. We also investigate variation in audit firm market share of a particular industry, and therefore, potential market power, over the 2000-2006 period as well. Our econometric model is estimated to gauge whether or not audit fees can be explained by changes in these concentration variables. Sullivan (2007) takes a different approach in addressing anticompetitive pricing, using auditor change (switching) data from 1988 to 2005 and similarly attributes audit fee increases to the new regulatory environment and increased effort on the part of auditors rather than anticompetitive behavior.[2] Asthana, et al. (2004) examines audit fess from 2000 to 2002 and concludes that the increase in the fee premium charged by the largest firms was the result of decreased competition in the audit market for multinational companies due to the exit of Arthur Andersen. However, as Sullivan (2007) points out, the authors cannot control for trends in audits fees that predate the Arthur Andersen dismantlement.[3]

Econometric Modeling Procedures for Handling Panel Data

Panel data provides potential advantages over pure cross sectional and pure time series designs and allows us to factor out the time- and space-invariant components of the data. As a result, panel data are able to identify and measure effects that are not detectable in other designs. There are two commonly accepted approaches to estimating panel data—the random-effects model and the fixed-effects model. In the fixed effects model individual effects are estimated, in this case, for each company to reflect the assumption that special features specific to each company—such as audit risk, management style, skill of internal auditors or audit committee, or internal control processes—can be captured best with a different, time-invariant intercept for each company. In a random effects model, in this context, these individual effects are captured through treating the intercept as a random variable with a unique error term for each company. While each model has its advantages and disadvantages, the random effects model is appropriate when we can plausibly assume that the individual effects (which are unobserved and unmeasured in the model) are uncorrelated with the explanatory variables that are measured and included in the model. Otherwise the fixed effects model is preferred, especially as a control for omitted variables bias, as it is in this context (see discussion below).

Using panel data—data across companies and over time—the basic model takes the form:

$$y_{it} = \theta + X_{it}\beta + Z_i\delta + \varepsilon_{it} \quad (1)$$

where y = the dependent variable (audit fees paid by the company to its auditor).

X = a matrix of explanatory variables that varies across time and individual companies. These are variables that help capture the characteristics of the public company client, the characteristics of the auditing industry, the characteristics of the auditor, and the characteristics of the audit engagement as well as variables that for control the effect of Sarbanes-Oxley.

Z = a matrix of variables that vary across companies but for each individual company are constant across the six years. The variables are essentially the variables that indicate the number of auditor changes over the period, indicate whether or not a company was a client of Arthur Andersen in 2002 as well as regional and industry dummy variables.

θ = constant term.

i = 1, 2, . . ., 12,749 and represents the individual companies in the initial panel.

t = 1, 2, . . ., 6 and represents the number of years (2000-2006).

As is the typical case with panel data, we have a large number of cross-sections (public companies) and a relatively small number of time periods. Therefore we specify the composite error structure for the disturbance term as follows:

$$\varepsilon_{it} = \alpha_i + \eta_{it} \quad (2)$$

where = company-specific error component which captures the unobserved heterogeneity across companies (either as a fixed- or random-effect).

$E(X_{it}\eta_{it}) = 0$ (there is no correlation between η_{it} and X_{it}).

The α_i is the individual effect which can be treated as either fixed or random. The fixed- and random-effect models which take account of the repetition inherent in the data and allow us to use the individual differences effectively.

Correspondingly, if we treat the individual effect as zero we can estimate the model using the simple ordinary least squares (OLS) procedure. This is a pooled OLS regression model where we assume the intercept and slope coefficients are constant across time and space and the normal error term (η_{it}) captures differences over time and individual companies. However, when the true model is random-effects model, pooling the observations in this manner using OLS produces biased estimates that are also not efficient when compared to the more complex generalized least squares (GLS) procedure (outlined below). Moreover, the pooled OLS model is also susceptible to omitted variables bias. Likelihood ratio tests strongly rejected the pooled OLS model in favor of the fixed-effects and therefore OLS would be inappropriate in this regard as well.

The random effects technique proceeds under the assumption that the ignorance about the unobserved differences in audit fees across companies is better captured through the disturbance term rather than the intercept. The random effects model basically maintains that the public companies in the sample have a common mean audit fee (represented by the constant term, θ) and that the individual differences in fees for each company are captured in the error term α_1[4] Given the composite nature of the new disturbance term which incorporates the individual random effect of each company, the appropriate method for producing estimates is GLS.[5] Feasible GLS derives an estimate of the covariance matrix of the error term and uses the information (heteroscedasticity from repeated observations of the same crosssection unit) to estimate the coefficients in the model.

The drawback to this approach is that it forces one to make the strong assumption that the unobserved random-effects are uncorrelated with the explanatory variables in the model $E(X_{it}\alpha_1) = 0$ in addition to the standard assumption $E(X_{it}\eta_{it}) = 0$). As a result, the random effect treatment of the panel data may also produce estimates that suffer from the inconsistency due to omitted variables. Therefore, the validity of the results would depend more heavily on the control variables included in the model to capture differences across companies, *unless* the omitted variables (unobserved heterogeneity across company) are uncorrelated with the concentration variables. If this is the case, the random-effect model may produce more appropriate estimates than the fixed-effects model. In our case, the Hausman test, which formally tests whether the omitted variables are correlated with the other regressors in the model, clearly rejected the random-effect model in favor of the fixed-effects model. Therefore, the results section of this appendix focuses primarily the fixed effects models (see below).

In the case of the fixed effects model, is estimated uniquely for each α_1 company as a fixed coefficient to be added to the intercept term. In this way, we take into the account the individuality of each company (each crosssectional unit) by letting the intercept vary by a fixed amount for each company. The benefit of the fixed effects estimator is that it is consistent in the presence of omitted variables. Because many variables that affect audit fees across companies are difficult to measure or could not be obtained this omission could bias the parameter estimates. With panel data and a fixed effect specification it is possible to obtain consistent estimates of the effect of concentration even when there are correlated omitted effects. The differences that exist across companies are essentially pulled out and accounted for explicitly, allowing for a more valid estimation of the effect of industry concentration on company audit fees. Moreover, in many cases the fixed effects estimates will still produce consistent estimates even when the random effects model is valid.

Variables Included in the Model

SEC disclosure requirements now require companies to disclose audit fees paid to the external auditor and that these fees paid be broken down into the following categories: (1) audit fees, (2) audit-related fees, (3) tax fees, and (4) all other fees.[6] Audit-related fees can include fees paid to the external auditor for due diligence services, internal control reviews or other work that is traditionally performed by the independent accountant. The dependent variable in our econometric models is total audit fees, which is composed of audit fees and audit-related fees. While the results we report below use this measure of fees, we also used audit fees (without audit-related fees) for each company in some models as a sensitivity test. More importantly, because SEC disclosure requirements were not in effect during 2000 and for a portion of 2001, some observations are based on firm-specific practices for categorizing fees rather than the more uniform categorization initiated by SEC regulations. We deal with this econometrically by dropping 2000 and 2001 in some specifications for sensitivity analysis, and, when these years are included, time fixed-effects are used to control for potential difference in the recording of audit fees.

The primary variables of interest are the industry concentration variables defined by two-digit North American Industry Classification System (NAICS) codes: (1) the share of the market held by a company's auditor of record in a given year in a given industry sector (*Sharef*) and (2) the Hirschman-Herfindahl Index (*HHI1*) for the industry sector in which the company operates in a given year. Both concentration variables are based on the total audit fees collected. The HHI is calculated by summing the squared market shares of all the firms auditing public company clients in a given industry. As table 9 illustrates, the HHI's computed for the various sectors of the economy vary across sectors over time. We also interacted the HHI variable with measures of company size, to allow for distinct effects for large and small companies. We did not include companies operating in the public administration sector in our econometric analysis as there were an insufficient number of companies to reliably determine concentration. Similarly, in some econometric specifications we dropped Agricultural and Warehousing companies as the numbers fell below 30 and 15 companies respectively in most years.

While the HHI variable captures the impact of overall concentration on audit fees, the market share variable can capture two distinct types of effects. One the one hand, market share can be an indicator of a firm's degree of monopoly power and large shares can give substantial market power to the firm if there are no significant competitors. On the other hand, high market share could result in economies of scale and lower costs which are then passed on to clients in the form of lower audit fees. In the case of the market for audit services the market share variable could also proxy for industry expertise (quality-differentiated services), which would justify higher fees. Therefore, a positive relationship between market share and audit fees would be consistent with both market power and an expertise or quality premium. We further explore this with a number of models to determine whether individual market power (monopolistic pricing) or industry expertise most likely explains the positive relationship we find between market share and audit fees (see results section).

Although, the fixed effect model guards against time invariant omitted variables bias, it is always advisable to explore possible causes of heterogeneity. We included a number of control variables in an attempt to capture the variation in audit fees across companies related to audit effort (size), risk factors and complexity. Table 10 includes a listing of the various variables included in the econometric models, ranging from company size (assets) to indicators of a restatement, a going concern opinion, negative earnings, late filings and controls for Sarbanes-Oxley (SOX). Sarbanes-Oxley added new costs to the standard audit, especially the Section 404 Report on internal controls in 2004.[7] Over the sample there are some companies that complete the yearly internal control review beginning in 2004 and other that do not. We controlled for this explicitly with a dummy variable, as well as an additional dummy if the company was found to have inadequate controls. As some of these variables may also be related to the concentration variables, controlling for them also enhances the internal validity of the parameter estimates.

Table 9. Hirchman-Herfindahl Indexes by Sector, 2000-2006

NAICS Sector	2000	2001	2002	2003	2004	2005	2006
Agriculture[a]	2,970	3,164	6,268	4,844	4,894	5,312	6,092
Mining	2,908	2,668	2,866	2,651	2,653	2,342	2,466
Utilities	2,837	3,321	4,508	3,848	3,870	3,751	3,680
Construction	2,233	2,665	3,188	3,184	3,091	3,079	3,042
Manufacturing: food processing and textiles	2,177	2,464	2,913	2,640	2,632	2,778	2,720
Manufacturing: wood, petroleum, minerals, chemical products	2,378	2,209	2,747	2,721	2,743	2,583	2,602
Manufacturing: durable	2,216	2,266	2,454	2,434	2,483	2,388	2,347
Wholesale trade	1,800	2,111	2,238	2,258	2,198	2,177	2,144
Traditional retail	1,767	2,483	2,553	2,497	2,431	2,559	2,558
Miscellaneous retail	2,643	2,253	2,434	2,414	2,429	2,286	2,207
Transportation	2,699	2,461	2,555	2,791	2,786	2,534	2,477
Warehousing[b]	4,036	3,154	3,364	3,273	3,567	3,259	3,601
Information	2,473	2,314	2,579	2,451	2,502	2,422	2,341
Finance and insurance	1,958	2,145	2,382	2,403	2,368	2,355	2,347
Real estate, rental and leasing	2,498	2,735	2,852	2,319	2,414	2,315	2,642
Professional, scientific, and technical	1,948	1,857	2,095	2,244	2,313	2,136	2,002
Management of companies and enterprises[c]	2,089	2,220	2,644	3,033	2,447	2,221	2,115
Administrative and support and waste management and remediation	5,215	2,923	2,372	2,417	2,352	2,343	2,201
Educational services	5,034	2,897	4,374	4,108	5,188	4,589	3,675
Health care and social assistance	3,654	2,701	3,920	3,163	2,872	2,786	2,689
Arts, entertainment, and recreation	2,194	1,896	1,956	1,954	2,252	1,798	2,029

Table 9. Hirchman-Herfindahl Indexes by Sector, 2000-2006 (Continued)

NAICS Sector	2000	2001	2002	2003	2004	2005	2006
Accommodation and food services	2,239	2,702	2,511	2,977	2,566	2,624	2,716
Other services	3,809	3,628	3,430	3,376	2,709	3,198	3,237
Public administration[d]	4,213	3,855	5,460	2,617	3,617	2,478	2,488
All sectors	1,999	2,034	2,392	2,393	2,413	2,333	2,300

Source: GAO analysis of Audit Analytics data.

Notes: Based on total audit fees collected in industries defined by two digit NAICS codes.

[a] The agriculture sector contains fewer than 30 companies.

[b] The warehousing sector contains fewer than 15 companies.

[c] The management of companies and enterprises sector comprises (1) establishments that hold the securities of companies and enterprises for the purpose of owning a controlling interest or influencing management decisions or (2) establishments that administer, oversee, and manage establishments of the company and that normally undertake the strategic or organizational planning and decision making role of the company or enterprise. Not included in any econometric specifications.

[d] Not included in any econometric specifications due to an insufficient number of companies.

Table 10. Primary Variables in the Econometric Analysis

Variable	Description
TAFEESADJ	Total audit and audit-related fees paid by a company to its auditor in 2006 dollars
ASSETSADJ	Assets of the audited company in 2006 dollars
BIGCO3	Indicates whether company has greater than $250 million in assets (2006 dollars).
BIGCO1	Indicates whether company has greater than $1 billion in assets (2006 dollars).
BIGCO35	Indicates whether company has greater than $3.5 billion in assets (2006 dollars).
HHI1	HHI (defined by total audit fees) for a sector defined by two-digit NAICS code
SHAREF	Percentage of the market (defined by audit fees) held by a company's auditor of record
LOSS	Indicates whether company experienced a loss in a given year
GC	Indicates concern about a company's ability to continue as a going concern was raised
RESTATDUM	Indicates whether a company filed restated financials during the year
LATE	Indicates whether a company filed a notice of nontimely filing during the year
INTERNAL	Indicates whether a company completed the Sarbanes-Oxley Act Section 404 review
INADEQ	Indicates whether companies internal control were found inadequate
POSTSOX	Indicates audit year occurs after the passage of the Sarbanes-Oxley Act
BUSY	Indicates whether the company's fiscal year end date occurs during the busy season (December)
CI (Client Influence)[a]	Measured as the fees paid by the company to a given audit firm relative to total fees paid by all clients audited by that firm in a given industry sector
EXPERT	Indicates whether a given firm audits 10 percent or more of all company clients audit in a particular industry sector
BIG45	Indicates whether a company is audited by one of the largest firms in a given year
MID4	Indicates whether a company is audited by a midsize firm in a given year
SEPARAUDITOR	Indicates whether the company paid additional audit-related fees to a second auditor
AUCH0006	Number of auditor switches for a given company over the 2000-2006 period
AACLIENT2002	Indicates whether a company switched from Andersen in 2002
Firm	Audit Firm specific dummy variables for the top eight firms
Year	Year dummy variables (period-fixed effects)
Region	Region dummy variables (Canada, Foreign and various section of the US)
Industry	Industry dummy variables (defined by two-digit NAICS codes)

Source: GAO.

[a] As pointed out in S. Bandyopadhyay and J. Kao, "Market Structure and Audit Fees: A Local Analysis," Contemporary Accounting Research, vol. 21, issue 3 (fall 2004), one might expect a dominant auditor to restrain any pricing behavior when faced with a powerful audit client, resulting in a diminished positive relation between auditor market concentration and audit fees. We include this variable to control for this possibility. Since, in the regressions below it is typically positive when it is significant—contrary to theoretical expectation—this variable could be a proxy for complexity.

Since accounting firms are now prohibited from providing services such as financial information system implementation and design, internal auditing, and a number of other services, any cross subsidization (or low-balling) of the audit that potentially existed in the early years (2000 and 2001) is less likely in the later years in our sample. Moreover, as indicated above, the sample consists of fees reported under the old SEC rules for 2000 and 2001, and fees reported under the new rule for 2002 through 2006. As a result, we also included time period fixed effects to control for regulatory changes, changes in the scope and complexity of audit engagements, changes in the manner in which, the audit was priced or audit fees were categorized and recorded, and other forces that can be captured by a company-invariant (consistent across companies) fixed effect. Collectively the variables and techniques help capture the characteristics, of the public company client (effect of the amount of effort required by the auditor), of the auditing industry (e.g., pricing differences across accounting firms), of the auditor (e.g., knowledge advantages due to specialization) and of the engagement (e.g., busy season) and help explain the variation in audit fees across companies. All appropriate variables were adjusted for inflation.

As table 11 shows there is a low degree of correlation between most of the explanatory variables in the panel. However, there is a high degree of correlation between the market share variable, the dummy indicating whether a firm is an industry expert and the dummy variable which indicates whether a company is audited by one of the largest accounting firms (Big 4/5 dummy variable). In fact, principal components analysis suggests the Big 4/5 dummy variable adds very little to a model once the market share variable is included.[8] As a result the Big 4/5 is not included in a given model if the market share variable is also being estimated. We also drop the expert variable in some specifications for sensitivity analysis in lieu of the somewhat high correlation with the market share and the interaction variables. It should be noted however, the correlation between HHI and market share is relatively low.

Table 11. Correlation Matrix, GAO Panel Data Set, Select Variables

	1	*2*	*3*	*4*	*5*	*6*	*7*	*8*	*9*	*10*	*11*	*12*	*13*	*14*	*15*
1. Log ASSETSADJ)	1.00														
2. LOSS	-0.43	1.00													
3. GC	-0.49	0.32	1.00												
4. POSTSOX	-0.03	-0.05	0.07	1.00											
5. BUSY	0.10	-0.02	-0.01	0.12	1.00										
6. CI	-0.26	0.11	0.19	0.04	-0.01	1.00									
7. EXPERT	0.53	-0.16	-0.31	-0.08	0.01	-0.36	1.00								
8. Log (HHI1)	0.07	-0.05	-0.03	0.20	0.01	0.02	0.08	1.00							
9. Log(HHI1)* BIGCO03	0.77	-0.38	-0.30	0.00	0.10	-0.21	0.40	0.06	1.00						
10. Log(SHAREF)	0.61	-0.20	-0.38	-0.10	0.02	-0.45	0.88	0.09	0.44	1.00					
11. INTERNAL	0.29	-0.17	-0.18	0.24	0.11	-0.09	0.18	0.01	0.28	0.22	1.00				
12. INADEQ	0.06	0.00	-0.04	0.07	0.02	-0.02	0.04	0.00	0.05	0.06	0.30	1.00			
13. LATE	-035	0.20	0.40	0.15	-0.06	0.19	-0.29	-0.01	-0.24	-0.33	-0.05	0.12	1.00		
14. RESTATDUM	-0.02	0.05	0.07	0.07	-0.03	0.04	-0.03	0.01	-0.02	-0.02	0.05	0.13	0.25	1.00	
15. BIG45	0.56	-0.17	-0.32	-0.11	0.02	-0.38	0.94	0.10	0.43	0.92	0.18	0.04	-0.31	-0.03	1.00

Source: GAO.

RESULTS

We ran roughly 100 different models, including several pooled OLS, random-effects and fixed-effects models with varied specifications as sensitivity tests. Given the number of issues that plague the simple OLS model and that formal tests strongly rejected the pooled OLS model in favor of fixed-effects, we do not report the pooled OLS results in this appendix. Moreover, since the Hausman test overwhelming rejected the random-effects in favor of the fixed-effect model, we present the results for the random-effects models for comparison only.[9] Note, also, that the time invariant variables (Zi), such as number of auditor changes over the period, and industry and region indicators appear in the random-effects model but not in the fixed-effects models as these variables are collinear with the unique fixed-effect estimated for each company. The random and fixed-effects models run on 2002 through 2006 data suggest that, in general, companies operating in more concentrated industries do not pay higher fees when other important drivers of audit fees are included (table 12). Moreover, focusing on the fixed-effect results, we found this result to hold even when we included 2000 and 2001 in the analysis or if we include only the post Sarbanes-Oxley years (2003-2006). In all cases, the HHI is positive but statistically insignificant.

To explore the differences between different size companies, we also interacted the HHI variable with a dummy variable that indicates whether a company exceeds $250 million in assets. This variable is both positive and significant, indicating that larger firms operating in more concentrated industries may pay higher fees, but we note that this effect is very small. Because this was an arbitrary definition which would include a number of companies considered small by other sources, we varied our definition of large using various cut-off values. When we defined large as $1 billion or $3.5 billion in assets the results remain the same. Consistently the estimates suggest that a 10 percent increase in the HHI for large companies results in an increase in audit fees around 0.5 percent. Since the dissolution of Andersen initiated an increase in the HHI by about 18 percent, the model suggests that the result on audit fees for the largest public companies would have been less than 1 percent.[10] By comparison the estimated effect of the 404 internal control requirements resulted in roughly a 45 percent increase in audit fees, while issuing a financial restatement is associated roughly with an 11 percent increase in fees. However, when we ran the models only on companies with assets greater than $250 million in assets (or any other sub-samples of large companies defined by assets) we found no relationship between industry concentration and audit fees for these companies. When we defined large by some measures we found a negative but statistically insignificant relationship between HHI and audit fees. Further, when we ran the model only on clients of the largest firms the coefficients on the interaction term were either much smaller (substantively insignificant) or statistically insignificant. As a result, this finding regarding the price impact for larger companies may not be robust and should be interpreted with caution.

The models also consistently show that accounting firms holding a larger market share of the industry in which the public company operates are found to charge higher fees (*Sharef* is statistically significant and positive in each instance) but this leaves open the question as to whether the empirical evidence is supportive of expertise-quality-differentiated services or anticompetitive pricing. Unfortunately, these are extremely difficult issues to address in a rigorous and comprehensive manner. Similar to other studies, we investigated the audit fee-market share relationship in various large and small client segments of the market. We found that market share-related price premium also exists in the small client segment of the market and these premiums were not statistically different from those that existed in the large company segment of the market (table 13).[11] Even when we ran the model on companies with assets below 100 million, we still found a statistically significant and positive relationship between the auditor's share of the market (Sharef) and audit fees. It should be noted that the HHI for this sector was well below the critical value of 1,000 in 2006. Therefore, the persistence of this positive relationship between market share and audit fees in all segments of the market—even those predisposed to perform competitively—suggest it is more likely due to industry or technical expertise (quality-differentiated service) and in the case of the larger firms, brand-name reputation.[12] A firm with industry expertise may exploit its specialization by developing and marketing audit-related services which are specific to clients in the industry and provide a higher level of assurance. If this is the case, such firms could earn a return on this investment by charging higher audit fees than other firms and remain competitive for the most relevant opportunities, even at a premium price. It should be noted that Oxera (2006), using similar modeling techniques, interpreted this association as an indicator of market power in U.K. audit markets but did not acknowledge the presence of quality differentiated services and industry expertise nor report any further investigation to unpack the relationship.[13]

Table 12. Random-Effects and Fixed-Effects Models Explaining Log of Fees

	Random Effects	Fixed Effects				$1 billion interaction term	$3.5 billion interaction term
	$ 250 million interaction term						
	2002 - 2006[a] N= 34,688	2000 - 2006 N= 43,239	2001 - 2006 N= 39,905	2002 - 2006 N= 34,703	2003 - 2006 N= 28,238	2001 - 2006 N= 39,905	2001 - 2006 N= 39,905
C	8.5647**	7.5929**	7.4699**	7.5436**	7.9463**	7.7733**	7.7827**
	(16.8464)	(21.6481)	(14.5038)	(11.2777)	(9.3876)	(15.3838)	(15.6559)
YEAR2001	——	0.1454**	——	——	——	——	——
		(14.8267)					
YEAR2002	——	0.3175**	0.1689**	——	——	0.1686**	0.1724**
		(18.8100)	(10.4579)			(10.4400)	(10.7074)
YEAR2003	0.1280**	0.4642**	0.3127**	0.1357**	——	0.3094**	0.3132**
	(16.2787)	(24.9257)	(17.6895)	(17.8404)		(17.4808)	(17.7304)
YEAR2004	0.3156**	0.6622**	0.5095**	0.3348**	0.1998**	0.5085**	0.5131**
	(36.2896)	(33.7899)	(27.4027)	(36.9703)	(24.1626)	(27.3279)	(27.6594)
YEAR2005	0.3722**	0.7426**	0.5861**	0.4088**	0.2724**	0.5850**	0.5906**
	(37.0582)	(37.1455)	(31.4034)	(37.0063)	(26.4758)	(31.3368)	(31.7133)
YEAR2006	0.3988**	0.7693**	0.6142**	0.4383**	0.3012**	0.6137**	0.6223**
	(36.8647)	(35.3901)	(30.0785)	(31.1552)	(22.4383)	(30.0751)	(30.5558)
LOG(ASSETSADJ)	0.2830**	0.2636**	0.2599**	0.2527**	0.2637**	0.2615**	0.2639**
	(122.2293)	(44.4466)	(42.3690)	(39.3751)	(35.9253)	(44.2531)	(45.5836)
LOSS	0.0398**	0.0363**	0.0337**	0.0299**	0.0278*	0.0269**	0.0213*
	(5.2908)	(4.6571)	(4.0579)	(3.1582)	(2.2360)	(3.2108)	(2.5405)
GC	0.1689**	0.1396**	0.1279**	0.1004**	0.1198**	0.1264**	0.1297**
	(13.8142)	(8.7037)	(7.5207)	(5.3223)	(5.1789)	(7.4163)	(7.5889)
POSTSOX	0.0823**	0.0697**	0.0685**	0.0691**	——	0.0717**	0.0703**
	(5.1217)	(4.6988)	(4.5681)	(4.2092)		(4.7615)	(4.6686)
BUSY	0.1085**	0.1314**	0.1362**	0.1302**	0.1184**	0.1346**	0.1339**
	(9.8573)	(4.3232)	(4.4531)	(4.1105)	(3.5753)	(4.4561)	(4.4427)

Table 12. (Continued).

	Random Effects	Fixed Effects				$1 billion interaction term	$3.5 billion interaction term
	$ 250 million interaction term						
	2002 - 2006[a] N= 34,688	2000 - 2006 N= 43,239	2001 - 2006 N= 39,905	2002 - 2006 N= 34,703	2003 - 2006 N= 28,238	2001 - 2006 N= 39,905	2001 - 2006 N= 39,905
CI	0.9475**	0.9034**	0.8999**	0.9147**	0.8870**	0.8835**	0.8854**
	(47.8395)	(31.5599)	(29.1252)	(25.9041)	(21.8819)	(28.9938)	(29.0351)
EXPERT	-0.4333**	-0.3211**	-0.3357**	-0.3818**	-0.3251**	-0.3375**	-0.3421**
	(-23.6342)	(-16.7375)	(-15.7221)	(-12.7964)	(-9.3465)	(-15.9276)	(-16.1688)
SEPARAUDITOR	0.0114	0.0348	0.0452	0.0531	0.0358	0.0494	0.0545
	(0.2679)	(0.7225)	(0.9213)	(1.0520)	(0.6314)	(1.0056)	(1.1057)
LOG(HHI1)	-0.0602	0.0199	0.0633	0.1001	0.0443	0.0295	0.0281
	(-0.9353)	(0.4521)	(0.9644)	(1.1852)	(0.4131)	(0.4595)	(0.4431)
LOG(HHI1)*BIGCO3	0.0559**	0.0386**	0.0437**	0.0502**	0.0503**	——	——
	(35.5015)	(15.2818)	(15.9620)	(15.9526)	(13.3452)		
LOG(HHI1)*BIGCO1	——	——	——	——	——	0.0502**	——
						(16.4422)	
LOG(HHI1)*BIGCO3 5	——	——	——	——	——	——	0.0664**
							(15.9693)
LOG(SHAREF)	0.2753**	0.2577**	0.2610**	0.2757**	0.2722**	0.2611**	0.2636**
	(71.2752)	(47.1572)	(44.0156)	(37.6615)	(32.4633)	(44.4352)	(44.5784)
INTERNAL	0.3870**	0.3644**	0.3655**	0.3663**	0.3667**	0.3542**	0.3564**
	(45.3539)	(40.1350)	(40.0650)	(38.6133)	(34.2462)	(38.7978)	(39.2137)
INADEQ	0.2043**	0.2488**	0.2183**	0.1811**	0.1568**	0.2306**	0.2308**
	(12.6448)	(13.0846)	(11.4915)	(9.4094)	(7.9006)	(12.2212)	(12.2179)
AACLIENT2002	-0.0203	——	——	——	——	——	——
	(-0.9367)						
LATE	0.1003**	——	——	0.0891**	0.0857**	——	——
	(11.7026)			(8.6441)	(7.3398)		
RESTATDUM	0.0926**	——	0.1050**	0.0759**	0.0668**	0.1024**	0.1018**
	(9.6802)		(9.8963)	(6.6881)	(5.3366)	(9.6697)	(9.6201)

Table 12. (Continued).

	Random Effects	Fixed Effects				$1 billion interaction term	$3.5 billion interaction term
	$ 250 million interaction term						
	2002 - 2006[a] N= 34,688	2000 - 2006 N= 43,239	2001 - 2006 N= 39,905	2002 - 2006 N= 34,703	2003 - 2006 N= 28,238	2001 - 2006 N= 39,905	2001 - 2006 N= 39,905
AUDCHS0006	-0.0014	——	——	——	——	——	——
	(-0.1862)						
Dummy variables							
Industry	Yes	No	No	No	No	No	No
Regional	Yes	No	No	No	No	No	No
Other statistics							
Hausman test of random effects model	862.9703	——	——	——	——	——	——
σ_e	0.4241	0.4271	0.4249	0.4264	0.4324	0.4242	0.4236
$R^{2\ b}$	0.8442	0.9345	0.9371	0.9397	0.9396	0.9373	0.9375
F-statistic	3999.2990	65.6400	63.4299	57.9157	47.9965	63.6369	63.8281
Durbin Watson Statistic	1.4526	1.7779	1.8756	2.0300	2.3273	1.8755	1.8745
Information criterion							
Akaike	——	1.3282	1.3307	1.3606	1.4210	1.3276	1.3247
Schwarz	——	3.2417	3.3817	3.6741	4.1530	3.3786	3.3757
Hannan-Quinn	——	1.9316	1.9800	2.0978	2.3001	1.9769	1.9740

Source: GAO.

Notes: T-statistics are in parentheses. * indicates significance at the 5 percent level and ** indicates significance at the 1 percent level.

aWhites' stacked covariance matrix was not used. In all other cases the covariance matrix was adjusted.

bAdjusted R2 is reported.

Table 13. Fixed Models Explaining Log of Fees, by Market Segments, 2001-2006

	Fixed effects: 2001-2006					
	>$250 million in assets N= 19,351	<$250 million in assets N= 20,554	>$500 million in revenue N= 11,815	> $1 billion in assets N= 10,433	< $1 billion in assets N= 29,472	< $0.1 billion in assets N= 15,918
C	3.4023**	10.2934**	6.1074**	5.3434**	9.4437**	10.3934**
	(4.4859)	(14.0739)	(6.5726)	(4.5316)	(16.1935)	(12.9132)
YEAR2002	0.1111**	0.2056**	0.1379**	0.1472**	0.1881**	0.1914**
	(5.0155)	(9.3704)	(5.2792)	(4.4616)	(10.6026)	(7.5918)
YEAR2003	0.2445**	0.3581**	0.2709**	0.2735**	0.3354**	0.3468**
	(10.2598)	(14.7338)	(9.5418)	(7.9036)	(17.0191)	(12.3685)
YEAR2004	0.4148**	0.5687**	0.4201**	0.4205**	0.5475**	0.5556**
	(16.2569)	(22.5425)	(13.5887)	(11.2816)	(26.5975)	(19.0359)
YEAR2005	0.4524**	0.6698**	0.4481**	0.4424**	0.6337**	0.6685**
	(17.4146)	(27.2448)	(13.9584)	(11.8177)	(30.9360)	(23.6873)
YEAR2006	0.4488**	0.7138**	0.4386**	0.4417**	0.6721**	0.7147**
	(15.7695)	(26.5128)	(12.4807)	(10.9920)	(30.0593)	(23.2328)
LOG(ASSETSADJ)	0.4650**	0.1589**	——	0.4799**	0.2051**	0.1331**
	(29.3864)	(26.5241)		(16.8403)	(33.5556)	(22.5666)
LOG(REVADJ)	——	——	0.4363**	——	——	——
			(17.8800)			
LOSS	0.0628**	0.0233*	0.0851**	0.0552**	0.0218*	0.0274*
	(5.4216)	(2.2515)	(6.3595)	(3.5098)	(2.3915)	(2.3546)
GC	0.0958*	0.0518**	0.0982*	0.1042	0.0884**	0.0249
	(2.2106)	(3.0334)	(2.0738)	(1.8025)	(5.1790)	(1.4470)
POSTSOX	0.1285**	-0.0038	0.1371**	0.1204**	0.0445**	-0.0178
	(6.2325)	(-0.1925)	(5.5588)	(4.0780)	(2.6985)	(-0.7790)
BUSY	-0.0071	0.2142**	0.2570**	0.0198	0.1798**	0.2502**
	(-0.1238)	(5.0299)	(3.1510)	(0.1909)	(5.0642)	(5.4635)

Table 13. (Continued).

	Fixed effects: 2001-2006					
	>$250 million in assets N= 19,351	<$250 million in assets N= 20,554	>$500 million in revenue N= 11,815	> $1 billion in assets N= 10,433	< $1 billion in assets N= 29,472	< $0.1 billion in assets N= 15,918
CI	1.5222**	0.8691**	2.3798**	2.1143**	0.8556**	0.9039**
	(18.0067)	(25.6574)	(14.0979)	(11.3065)	(27.4069)	(24.6155)
EXPERT	-0.1889**	-0.6588**	-0.1056**	-0.1166**	-0.4559**	-0.8101**
	(-7.3891)	(-18.8267)	(-3.2930)	(-3.5222)	(-17.4709)	(-18.9266)
SEPARAUDITOR	0.0469	0.0098	-0.0082	-0.1107	0.0404	-0.0198
	(0.4328)	(0.1743)	(-0.0422)	(-0.4357)	(0.8328)	(-0.3128)
LOG(HHI1)	0.0670	-0.0537	-0.1748	-0.2262	-0.0566	-0.0035
	(0.7349)	(-0.5658)	(-1.8132)	(-1.7274)	(-0.7589)	(-0.0339)
LOG(SHAREF)	0.2540**	0.2913**	0.3430**	0.2686**	0.2714**	0.3105**
	(24.3212)	(36.5375)	(15.1644)	(15.6734)	(40.9955)	(33.9122)
INTERNAL	0.3878**	0.4562**	0.3663**	0.3418**	0.4395**	0.4680**
	(33.6500)	(27.6471)	(26.3227)	(22.6297)	(38.7850)	(19.8015)
INADEQ	0.1882**	0.2132**	0.2188**	0.1661**	0.2353**	0.1980**
	(8.9729)	(6.0029)	(9.0037)	(6.2371)	(10.4055)	(3.2663)
RESTATDUM	0.1066**	0.1105**	0.0886**	0.0988**	0.1099**	0.1168**
	(7.9981)	(7.5543)	(5.8784)	(5.7273)	(9.0035)	(7.1903)
Dummy variables						
Industry	No	No	No	No	No	No
Region	No	No	No	No	No	No
Other statistics						
σ_2	0.3484	0.4110	0.3212	0.3193	0.4129	0.4041
$R^{2\,a}$	0.9384	0.8879	0.9244	0.9365	0.9052	0.8762
F-statistic	60.9300	28.0144	46.9472	54.9306	36.8678	23.5043
Durbin Watson Statistic	1.8034	2.1176	1.8467	1.8216	2.0067	2.1538
Information criterion						
Akaike	0.9443	1.2987	0.7896	0.7820	1.2917	1.2768

Table 13. (Continued).

	Fixed effects: 2001-2006					
	>$250 million in assets N= 19,351	<$250 million in assets N= 20,554	>$500 million in revenue N= 11,815	> $1 billion in assets N= 10,433	< $1 billion in assets N= 29,472	< $0.1 billion in assets N= 15,918
Schwarz	2.9466	3.6239	2.7545	2.7668	3.4984	3.6906
Hannan-Quinn	1.6005	2.0584	1.4492	1.4524	2.0003	2.0754

Source: GAO.

Notes: T-statistics are in parentheses; * indicates significance at the 5 percent level and ** indicates significance at the 1 percent level. Whites' stacked covariance matrix was used in all specifications.

[a] Adjusted R^2 is reported.

We conducted a number of sensitivity test to examine the robustness of our findings. For example, we used the log of audit fees—net of audit-related fees—as the dependent variable and obtained similar results. To investigate whether multicollinearity was an issue, we ran a number of models excluding the potentially collinear variables and obtained similar results. We also altered the functional form, using market share instead of logged market share, and obtained results which more strongly supported our initial results. Because estimated coefficients of the fee determinants could differ significantly for the largest and other auditors, we also ran the model separately for these two classes of firms. To address potential problems of endogeneity we estimated the relationships using two-stage least squares. Finally, to investigate whether the results were sensitive to unbalanced nature of the data—the number of companies in the sample for each industry differs across the years—we estimated the model using sample probability weights, where the weights are based on the number of companies in a given industry (or alternatively total revenues, fees paid or assets). In our case, this amounted to de-meaning the data to obtain the fixed effects estimates and then running weighted least squares. Consistently, we found no evidence of a positive and significant relationship between industry concentration and audit fees.

While our analysis suggests the increase in audit fees appears largely unrelated to supplier concentration, it is difficult to determine the extent to which audit pricing is consistent with competitive behavior with the available data because of all the contemporaneous changes occurring in the market. As a result these results should be interpreted with a consideration of a number of limitations. First, this is an aggregate analysis and, therefore, does not demonstrate that all companies receive a competitive price (local markets may be important). Moreover, the absence of evidence of uncompetitive pricing does not necessarily imply that we can conclude that the market is competitive from a pricing perspective. Second, our results are based on one battery of tests focused on *industry* (*economic sector*) concentration and this does not imply that it is the definitive way to examine the effect of concentration on prices. While evidence suggests that some sectors have particularly complex audits and sector-specific expertise is an important determinant of auditor choice many companies are involved in activities that cut across multiple industries raising some questions about characterizing industry-specific markets as unique audit markets, especially for large firms. Our investigation was undertaken because it appeared to be a useful way to consider the effect of concentration given the available data. Additional data may allow for analysis that may address the issue more completely or more validly. Third, although the fixed effect estimator is robust to the omission of any relevant time-invariant variables and we have explained over 90 percent of the variation in fees, if there are time-varying differences that have been omitted, the results could be biased. As complexity and inherent risk of the individual client audits could vary over time there is some concern that financial variables traditionally included in the literature could not be included here (e.g. number of subsidiaries, inventory and receivables). However, this threat should be balanced against the power of the fixed-effects estimator which may capture some of this effect.

Fourth, our conclusion that quality-differentiation and industry expertise most likely better explains market dynamics than monopolistic pricing, while standard in the academic literature, critically hinges on the smaller company segment actually performing competitively. We, like others, have made this assumption based on the low HHI statistics computed for that segment of the market and other market indicators that suggest competitive pricing for smaller companies. Users of this report should note that our tests of individual market power were limited and the results should be interpreted in light of this limitation. Fifth, potential measurement error in the audit fee variable, assuming it is random, would make it more likely that we would conclude that a relationship does not exist when indeed it does. Given the large amount of the variation in fees we have explained and the techniques we have used, this (statistical validity) would not appear to be an issue.

REFERENCES

[1] For the purpose of this report, public companies are defined as those that are listed on the American Stock Exchange (Amex), NASDAQ, or the New York Stock Exchange (NYSE) or whose stock is traded off these exchanges—for example, through OTC Bulletin Board (OTCBB), excluding funds, trusts, nonoperating companies, or subsidiaries of another public company. Large public companies generally include those on the Fortune 1000 list, unless otherwise noted.

[2] The 8 largest firms in the 1980s were Arthur Andersen LLP, Arthur Young LLP, Coopers and Lybrand LLP, Deloitte Haskins and Sells LLP, Ernst and Whinney LLP, Peat Marwick Mitchell LLP, Price Waterhouse LLP, and Touche Ross LLP. For the purposes of this report, the largest firms include Deloitte and Touche LLP, Ernst and Young LLP, KPMG LLP, and PricewaterhouseCoopers LLP. In our 2003 report on consolidation and competition, we referred to this group as the "top tier" based on revenue and staff size. See GAO, *Public Accounting Firms: Mandated Study on Consolidation and Competition*, GAO-03-864 (Washington, D.C.: July 30, 2003). In our mandated study on audit firm rotation, we defined Tier 1 as firms with 10 or more public company clients. See GAO, *Public Accounting Firms: Required Study on the Potential Effects of Mandatory Audit Firm Rotation*, GAO-04-216 (Washington, D.C.: Nov. 21, 2003).

[3] The largest firms each audited more than 1,200 public companies for 2006 according to Public Accounting Report. These firms are commonly referred to as the "Big 4" firms.

[4] The midsize firms—BDO Seidman LLP, Crowe Chizek and Company LLC, Grant Thornton LLP, and McGladrey and Pullen LLP—each audited more

than 100 but fewer than 425 public companies for 2006 and had around $1 billion in revenue or less according to Public Accounting Report.

[5] In addition, a large number of accounting firms have no public company clients.

[6] GAO, Public Accounting Firms: Mandated Study on Consolidation and Competition, GAO-03-864 (Washington, D.C.: July 30, 2003).

[7] Sarbanes-Oxley Act of 2002, Pub. L. No. 107-204, 116 Stat. 745 (July 30, 2002).

[8] Our initial population included over 6,900 U.S.-based public companies that traded on major exchanges (NYSE, NASDAQ, AMEX, OTCBB). Company estimates throughout the report do not include funds, trusts, nonoperating companies, or subsidiaries of another public company.

[9] According to these criteria, approximately 872 companies are large, 3,212 companies are midsize, and 2,822 companies are small.

[10] Unless otherwise noted, results from our public company survey are representative of and generalized to the larger public company population our sample was drawn from.

[11] Unless otherwise noted, accounting firm survey results do not include the responses of the largest firms or firms with four or fewer audit clients. Also, data for smaller firms refer to survey respondents only and cannot be generalized to all smaller firms because of lower response rates for this group.

[12] SEC Release No. 33-8183, Strengthening the Commission's Requirements Regarding Auditor Independence, 68 Fed. Reg. 6006 (Feb. 5, 2003).

[13] In May 2005, the Supreme Court reversed the criminal conviction of Arthur Andersen. *Arthur Andersen LLP v. United States*, 544 U.S. 696 (2005).

[14] Sarbanes-Oxley Act of 2002, Pub. L. No. 107-204, 116 Stat. 745 (July 30, 2002).

[15] Pub. L. No. 107-204, § 107, 116 Stat. 745, 765.

[16] An issuer is a company that issues or proposes to issue securities that are registered under section 12 of the Securities Exchange Act of 1934 (15 U.S.C. § 78l) or that is required to file reports under section 15(d) (15 U.S.C. § 78o(d)), or that files or has filed a registration statement that has not yet become effective under the Securities Act of 1933 (15 U.S.C. § 77a et seq.) and that it has not withdrawn.

[17] See PCAOB Release No. 2005-023, Report on the Initial Implementation of Auditing Standard No. 2, An Audit of Internal Control Over Financial Reporting Performed in Conjunction with an Audit of Financial Statements (Nov. 30, 2005); PCAOB Release No. 2007-001, Observations on Auditors'

Implementation of PCAOB Standards Relating to Auditors' Responsibilities with Respect to Fraud (Jan. 22, 2007); PCAOB Release No. 2007-004, Report on the Second-Year Implementation of Auditing Standard No. 2, An Audit of Internal Control over Financial Reporting Performed in Conjunction with an Audit of Financial Statements (Apr. 18, 2007); and PCAOB Release No. 2007-010, Report on the PCAOB's 2004, 2005, and 2006 Inspections of Domestic Triennially Inspected Firms (Oct. 22, 2007).

[18] Section 302 specifically requires an officer to certify that he or she has reviewed the report and that, based on his or her knowledge, the report does not contain any untrue statement; the certifying officers are responsible for internal controls; they have made certain disclosures to the audit committee; and, they have indicated any significant changes to internal controls subsequent to the date of their evaluation. SEC Release No. 33-8124, *Certification of Disclosure in Companies' Quarterly and Annual Reports*, 67 Fed. Reg. 57276 (Sept. 9, 2002).

[19] SEC Release No. 33-8238, Management's Report on Internal Control Over Financial Reporting and Certification of Disclosure in Exchange Act Periodic Reports, 68 Fed. Reg. 36636 (June 18, 2003).

[20] SEC defines a public company as an accelerated filer if it meets two conditions. First, it must have a public float of $75 million or more as of the last business day of its most recently completed second fiscal quarter. Second, it must have filed at least one annual report with the SEC. Initially accelerated filers were required to file for years ending after June 15, 2004, but SEC granted an extension to November 15, 2004. See SEC Release No. 33-8392, *Management's Report on Internal Control over Financial Reporting and Certification of Disclosure in Exchange Act Periodic Reports*, 69 Fed. Reg. 9722 (Mar. 1, 2004).

[21] SEC Press Release No. 2007-123.

[22] A tight oligopoly is generally defined as a market in which four providers hold over 60 percent of the market and other firms face significant barriers to entry into the market.

[23] The Hirschman-Herfindahl Index is one of the concentration measures that government agencies, including the Department of Justice (DOJ) and the Federal Trade Commission, use when assessing concentration to enforce U.S. antitrust laws.

[24] We found that the Mid-Atlantic and Midwest regional audit markets were somewhat more concentrated than the western regions, although all regional audit markets were highly concentrated.

[25] GAO-03-864, 12-15.

[26] Figures do not include a number of companies with missing financial data. The category of companies with greater than $1 billion in revenue roughly corresponds to the Fortune 1000 list. In 2006, the smallest company on the Fortune 1000 list had revenues just over $1.4 billion. As a result, the $1 billion and over segment shown in the figure includes the Fortune 1000, as well as other large companies.

[27] For the remainder of this report, we define large companies as those that are members of the Fortune 1000, midsize companies as those that have market capitalization of $75 million or greater but are not in the Fortune 1000, and small companies as those with market capitalization of less than $75 million. Using this definition, 12.6 percent of the 6,906 companies in our survey population are large, 46.5 percent are midsize, and 40.9 percent are small.

[28] Unless otherwise noted, the margin of error for public company survey results was less than 12 percentage points.

[29] Sections 201 and 2(a)(8) of the Sarbanes-Oxley Act. Nonaudit services are any professional services provided to a company by a registered public accounting firm, other than those provided to a company in connection with an audit or a review of the company's financial statements.

[30] The most common reasons large companies reported for retaining their current auditor included satisfaction with their current auditor, that auditor's technical expertise compared with other firms, and the burden of changing auditors. See http://www.gao.gov/cgi-bin/getrpt?GAO-08-164SP for more detailed survey results.

[31] The survey for our 2003 report was sent to a random sample of Fortune 1000 companies to collect information on their experiences with their auditors of record. The response rate for this survey was 64 percent, but the results were not generalizable to the population of large public companies. See GAO, *Accounting Firm Consolidation: Selected Large Public Company Views on Audit Fees, Quality, Independence, and Choice*, GAO-03-1158 (Washington, D.C.: Sept. 30, 2003).

[32] Appendix II contains more information on concentration by industry sector.

[33] The difference in the percentage of large domestic and large multinational companies indicating that the choice of accounting firms was inadequate was not significant.

[34] The data on auditor changes indicate that large companies change auditors less frequently than midsize and smaller companies. Between 2003 and 2006, there were approximately 28 changes per year per 1000 companies among large companies, 84 changes per year per 1000 companies among

midsize companies, and 264 changes per year per 1000 companies among small companies.

[35] Our analysis is based on a panel data set compiled for over 12,000 companies from 2000 through 2006. The panel data set allowed us to exploit a number of techniques to increase the validity of the results, including estimating "random-effect" and "fixed-effect" model specifications. The fixed-effects model helps to control for the potentially large number of unmeasured forces that might explain the differences in the audit fees paid across public companies. As a result, the fixed-effects models were able to account for over 90 percent of the variation in audit fees. Time period fixed effects were added to help control for Sarbanes-Oxley and other factors that have impacted the fees paid by all public companies. See appendix V for a more complete discussion of our econometric approach, including model specification, variables used, data sources, estimation techniques, and limitations.

[36] We ran a model with small and large companies and included a variable that allowed us to differentiate the effect of concentration from larger companies.When the smallest companies were excluded from the analysis, we did not find an effect of concentration on fees for the remaining companies. See appendix V for limitations.

[37] Appendix V includes the various limitations of our data and the model we developed.

[38] Since price competition is assumed to prevail in the small client segment of the audit market because of its low concentration, any premium from the effect of market power should be competed away. However, premiums that exist due to brand name reputation or quality-differentiated services will not be. A number of academic studies on publicly traded U.S. firms also explained sizeable premiums for the big accounting firms as the result of product differentiation and brand-name reputation and not of market power. For a summary see, David Hay, W. Robert Knechel, and Norman Wong, "Audit Fees: A Meta-analysis of the Effect of Supply and Demand Attributes," *Contemporary Accounting Research*, vol. 23, no. 1 (spring 2006).

[39] One objective of the Sarbanes-Oxley Act was to improve auditor independence and audit quality through stricter limitation on nonaudit services, the establishment of the PCAOB and its inspection program, and requirements that auditors assess and report on internal controls over financial reporting at public companies.

[40] Six cases were reported in *Aon Professional Risks*, "Awards/Settlements: Analysis of a Selection of Publicly Known Matters Involving Auditors," (Montreal, Canada: March 2006.) Some of the reported settlements might not have been approved by the courts, and some of the reported awards may have been appealed. Four other cases, the Andersen settlement in the Sunbeam case, KPMG settlements involving Rite Aid and Lernout and Hauspie, and a PricewaterhouseCoopers settlement in the Tyco International case, were widely reported. For these cases, see In re Sunbeam Securities Litigation, Case No. 98-8258-CIV-Middlebrooks, USDC SDNY, Order Approving Settlement (Nov. 29, 2001); In re Rite Aid Securities Litigation, 146 F. Supp. 2d 706 (E.D. Pa. 2001); In re Lernout and Hauspie Securities Litigation, Civ. Act. No. 00-CV-11589 (PBS), USDC Mass, Order and Final Judgment; In re Tyco Securities Litigation, Stipulation of Settlement, MDL Docket 02-1335-PB, Civ. Case No. 02-866-PB (July 6, 2007). One research organization examined class action securities fraud filings against companies in general and noted that new filings, including those that allege specific accounting allegations (to the extent they could be identified in complaints and/or press releases), have generally declined since 2004. See Cornerstone Research, *Securities Class Action Case Filings, 2007 Mid-Year Assessment* (July 2007) and Cornerstone's previous yearly reports.

[41] See, for example, Lawrence A. Cunningham, "Too Big to Fail: Moral Hazard in Auditing and the Need to Restructure the Industry Before It Unravels," 106 *Columbia Law Review* 1698 (2006).

[42] Regulators from outside the United States, including those from Australia, Canada, and the European Union, had also begun investigations of the proposed merger.

[43] In this simulation, we assumed that surviving firms would keep all of their current clients even after picking up clients from the failed firm. If some firms would shed clients to midsize or smaller firms as they add clients from the failed firm, the effect on concentration could be lower.

[44] SEC Release No. 33-8070, *Requirements for Arthur Andersen LLP Auditing Clients*, 67 Fed. Reg. 13518 (Mar. 22, 2002).

[45] Accounting firm survey data in this report does not include the responses of the largest firms, or firms with four or fewer audit clients unless otherwise noted. Also, data for smaller firms refer to survey respondents only and cannot be generalized to all smaller firms because of low response rates for this group.

[46] Fifty percent of midsize firms and 75 percent of smaller firms we surveyed said that they were not interested in serving as auditor for additional large public companies.

[47] Public company survey statistics are accurate within 12 percentage points, unless otherwise noted.

[48] We did not evaluate PCAOB's inspection program for this report.

[49] Auditor independence is a frequently cited concern about alternative practice structures, and the American Institute of Certified Public Accountants (AICPA) has established additional independence rules for them to ensure that attest services can be performed with objectivity and will protect the public interest.

[50] The International Ethics Standards Board for Accountants, an independent standard-setting body within the International Federation of Accountants released an exposure draft, *Code of Ethics for Professional Accountants,* for comment in December 2006.

[51] Unless otherwise noted, the margin of error for public company survey results was less than 12 percentage points.

[52] Large companies were more likely than small and midsize companies to retain their auditor for at least 10 years (47 percent and 20 percent, respectively).

[53] Accounting firm survey data in this report does not include the responses of the largest firms, or firms with four or fewer audit clients unless otherwise noted. Also, data for smaller firms refer to survey respondents only and cannot be generalized to all smaller firms because of low response rates for this group.

[54] See GAO, Public Accounting Firms: Required Study on the Potential Effects of Mandatory Audit Firm Rotation, GAO-04-216 (Washington, D.C.: Nov. 21, 2003).

[55] The partner rotation requirements went into effect May 6, 2003.

[56] The Financial Reporting Council oversees the regulatory activities of the professional accountancy and actuarial bodies in the United Kingdom. In October 2006, the Market Participants Group was established to advise the council on possible actions that market participants could take to mitigate the risks arising from the characteristics of the market for public company audits in the U.K.. In October, 2007, the group issued a report, titled *Choice in the UK Audit Market, Final Report of the Market Participants Group*, which contains 15 recommendations to increase auditor choice in the United Kingdom.

[57] This survey was to a random sample of Fortune 1000 companies on their experiences with their auditors of record. See GAO, *Accounting Firm Consolidation: Selected Large Public Company Views on Audit Fees, Quality, Independence, and Choice*, GAO-03-1158 (Washington, D.C.: Sept. 30, 2003).

[58] GAO-03-864.

[59] U.S. Senator Charles Schumer and New York City Mayor Michael Bloomberg commissioned the management consulting firm McKinsey and Company to work with the New York City Economic Development Corporation to develop the report *Sustaining New York's and the U.S.' Global Financial Services Leadership* (2006).

[60] In 2007, charges against 13 of the individuals were dismissed by the court, and these dismissals have been appealed by the government.

[61] Samuel A. DiPiazza and others, Global Capital Markets and The Global Economy: A Vision From the CEOs of the International Audit Networks (November 2006), available at http://www.globalpublicpolicy ymposium.com.

[62] According to AICPA and the National Association of State Boards of Accountancy (NASBA), all 50 states and the District of Columbia have adopted the Uniform Accountancy Act's ownership provisions, which require CPAs to be the majority owners of audit firms, or stricter ownership provisions. The Uniform Accountancy Act is a model for state board legislation developed by the AICPA and NASBA. It is nonbinding, and states may adopt it voluntarily, in whole or in part.

[63] We asked firms for their views on the effectiveness of a list of possible measures. Results showed that responses varied on whether the following were at least somewhat effective: merger/acquisition (71 percent); access to specialized technical and industry expertise (63 percent); liability/tort reform (61 percent); participation in an affiliation (56 percent); alternative practice structures (25 percent); mandatory audit firm rotation (44 percent); ability to raise capital (32 percent); regulatory changes (25 percent). See also GAO-08-164SP for detailed survey results.

[64] We did not evaluate the effectiveness of these programs for this report.

[65] AICPA has several mechanisms to support CPAs and firms that audit public companies, including the Accounting and Auditing hotline and the Center for Audit Quality (CAQ). AICPA and the largest public accounting firms established the CAQ, an autonomous public policy organization that is affiliated with AICPA. The CAQ's mission is to foster confidence in the audit process. To help fulfill that mission, the CAQ provides technical

support for public company auditing professionals through web casts, conference calls, briefings, and alerts on public company auditing developments and practices.

Appendix I

[1] See appendix V for more details on audit fees and disclosure requirements.

Appendix II

[1] See appendix V for more details on audit fees and disclosure requirements.
[2] Data on audit revenue from the *Public Accounting Report* include revenue from audits of both public and private companies. Unless otherwise noted, market shares and other concentration measures in this report are based on audits of public companies only.
[3] HHI calculated based on Audit Analytics audit fee database by summing the squares of the individual market shares of all the firms within a given market. For example, a market consisting of five firms with market shares of 35 percent, 30 percent, 20 percent, and 10 percent has an HHI of 2625 (352 + 302 + 202 + 102). The HHI reflects both the market shares of the top firms and the composition of the market outside of the top firms, whereas the four-firm concentration ratio does not.
[4] A study by London Economics in 2006 for the European Commission found that the audit market HHI in the UK and member countries of the European Union varied widely but were generally higher than the HHI threshold of 2000 used by the European Union as indicating a market where a merger could create competitive concerns. See London Economics in association with Ralf Ewert, "Study on the Economic Impact of Auditors' Liability Regimes," *Final Report to EC-DG Internal Market and Services* (Frankfurt am Main, Germany, September 2006) and *Official Journal of the European Union*, "Guidelines on the assessment of horizontal mergers under the Council Regulation on the control of concentrations between undertakings," 2004/C31/03 (May 2, 2004).
[5] This does not imply GAO advocates defining the audit market this way, rather this segmentation suggests some differences that might be relevant for analyzing choice and other competition-related matters. Only if we can define industry-specific markets and regional markets as unique audit

market sectors of the economy is such a characterization appropriate. Evidence suggests that some sectors have particularly complex audits and sector-specific expertise is an important determinant of auditor choice. This should be viewed in light of the fact that many companies are involved in activities that cut across multiple industries.

[6] According to some, local concentration measures may be more appropriate than national measures because the availability of professional accounting, advertising and law services depends on the location of personnel.

[7] The scenarios are based on simple assumptions and the estimates for the increases in the HHI are for illustrative purposes only.

Appendix III

[1] Foreign companies, benefit plans, pension, health, and welfare funds, subsidiaries with parents already included, and fund and trust entities are not included in this analysis.

[2] See http://www.gao.gov/cgi-bin/getrpt?GAO-08-164SP for full results to this survey question.

[3] We also reviewed the reasons for auditor changes in the Audit Analytics auditor change database. Reasons such as independence issues, fee reductions, accounting firm merging or exiting the market were also cited in these data.

Appendix IV

[1] The results from our public company survey are representative of and generalized to the larger public company population our sample was drawn from. Unless otherwise noted, the margin of error for public company survey results was less than 12 percentage points.

[2] In our 2003 study on the potential effects of mandatory audit firm rotation mandated by the Sarbanes-Oxley Act (GAO-04-216), we defined a quality audit as one in which the auditor conducts the audit in accordance with *Generally Accepted Auditing Standards* (GAAS) to provide reasonable assurance that the audited financial statements and related disclosures are (1) presented in accordance with *Generally Accepted Accounting Principles* (GAAP) and (2) are not materially misstated whether due to errors or fraud. This definition assumes that reasonable third parties with knowledge of the

relevant facts and circumstances would have concluded that the audit was conducted in accordance with auditing standards and, that within the requirements of those auditing standards, the auditor appropriately detected and then dealt with known material misstatements by (1) ensuring that appropriate adjustments, related disclosures, and other changes were made to the financial statements to prevent them from being materially misstated, (2) modifying the auditor's opinion on the financial statements if appropriate changes or other adjustments were not made, or (3) if warranted, resigning as the public company's auditor of record and reporting the reasons for the resignation to SEC.

[3] Section 104(d) (2) of the Sarbanes-Oxley Act.

[4] The AICPA peer review program is still applicable for PCAOB inspected firms' non-SEC issuer audit and accounting practices.

[5] Accounting firm survey data in this report does not include the responses of the largest firms, or firms with four or fewer audit clients unless otherwise noted. Also, data for smaller firms refer to survey respondents only and cannot be generalized to all smaller firms because of low response rates for this group.

[6] Section 301 of the Sarbanes-Oxley Act requires the audit committee to be responsible for hiring, compensating, and overseeing the work of the accounting firm.

[7] The aspects of audit quality we asked about were (1) responsiveness to client questions and needs, (2) technical capability with accounting principles and auditing standards, (3) amount of time spent by audit engagement team, (4) amount of time spent by senior partners and experts, (5) appropriate time spent on issues based on risk areas, (6) experience and capability of engagement partner, (7) experience and capability of engagement staff, (8) addition of audit of internal control over financial reporting, and (9) ability/willingness to identify and surface material reporting issues.

Appendix V

[1] The manner in which audit fees are categorized and reported has changed since 2000 as well. As discussed below, companies were required to report fees paid to their external auditor more uniformly in 2001.

[2] Mary Sullivan, "Great Migration: How Recent Events Changed the Switching Behavior of Top-Tier Audit Clients" (George Washington

University working paper, Washington, D.C., July 2007). While this approach allows for a longer-term look at the audit market, it can only investigate whether auditor switching changed as a result of Andersen's dismantlement relative to other factors such as the Sarbanes-Oxley Act. Auditor switching behavior may reasonably be interpreted as an indicator of pricing behavior but it does not directly address whether audit fees are higher or lower due to concentration.

[3] See Sharad Asthana et al, "The Effect of Enron, Andersen, and Sarbanes-Oxley on the Market for Audit Services" (SSRN Working Paper, June 2004), http://ssrn.com/abstract=560963. This is one of the reasons we do not attempt a pure interrupted time series design using audit fees. Audit fees data were not publicly available until recently, and, as a result, our data source did not have fee data prior to 2000. Moreover, it would be difficult to reach a valid conclusion since the dismantlement of Andersen occurred around the same time as the passage of the Sarbanes-Oxley Act.

[4] The random effects model can be thought of as a regression with a random constant term. In other words, it is assumed that the intercept is a random outcome variable that is a function of a mean value plus a random error.

[5] Because α_1 is in the composite error for each time period t, the error term (serially correlated across time, invalidating OLS estimates.

[6] In November 2000, the SEC adopted a rule requiring public companies to disclose audit and audit-related fees paid to their outside auditors. These requirements were later expanded to include a uniform categorization of fees, among other things.

[7] Although compliance was not initially anticipated until 2004 for large companies or 2005 for smaller companies (before being later delayed), it is likely that 2003 fees include some Section 404 attestation costs in preparation for full compliance.

[8] Principal components analysis involves a mathematical procedure that transforms a number of possibly correlated variables into a small number of uncorrelated variables called principal components. The first principal component accounts for as much as the variability in the data as possible, and each succeeding component accounts for as much as the remaining variability as possible. In our case the market share variable accounts for 96 percent of the variance in the factor space.

[9] Additionally, the random effects model allows us to attempt to separate out the partial effects of the time invariant variables.

[10] For individual sectors this result could vary. For example, since the dissolution of Arthur Andersen led to an increase in the HHI by about 36

percent in the utilities sector, the model suggests the resultant impact on audit fees for large companies (with over $1 billion in assets or revenue) in this sector would have been roughly 1.8 percent. Either way this is a very small especially when viewed as a percentage of large company assets or revenue.

[11] Since price competition is assumed to prevail in the small client segment of the audit market because of its low concentration, any premium existing due to the effect of market power should be competed away but premiums that exist due to brand name reputation or quality-differentiated services will not.

[12] This interpretation of the premium accruing to larger firms is commonplace in the academic literature on audit fees.

[13] Competition and Choice in the UK Audit Market," *Oxera* (April 2006).

INDEX

A

B

C

D

E

F

G

N

O

P

Q

R

S

T

U

V

W